Ceres' Runaway

Alice Meynell

Contents

CERES' RUNAWAY	7
A VANQUISHED MAN	10
A NORTHERN FANCY	14
LAUGHTER	18
HARLEQUIN MERCUTIO	22
THE LITTLE LANGUAGE	24
ANIMA PELLEGRINA!	28
THE SEA WALL	32
THE DAFFODIL	38
ADDRESSES	42
THE AUDIENCE	45
TITHONUS	47
THE TOW PATH	52
THE TETHERED CONSTELLATIONS	55
POPULAR BURLESQUE	57
DRY AUTUMN	60
THE PLAID	64
TWO BURDENS	66
THE UNREADY	70
THE CHILD OF TUMULT	74
THE CHILD OF SUBSIDING TUMULT	79

CERES' RUNAWAY

BY

Alice Meynell

CERES' RUNAWAY

One can hardly be dull possessing the pleasant imaginary picture of a Municipality hot in chase of a wild crop--at least while the charming quarry escapes, as it does in Rome. The Municipality does not exist that would be nimble enough to overtake the Roman growth of green in the high places of the city. It is true that there have been the famous captures--those in the Colosseum, and in the Baths of Caracalla; moreover a less conspicuous running to earth takes place on the Appian Way, in some miles of the solitude of the Campagna, where men are employed in weeding the roadside. They slowly uproot the grass and lay it on the ancient stones--rows of little corpses--for sweeping up, as at Upper Tooting; one wonders why. The governors of the city will not succeed in making the Via Appia look busy, or its stripped stones suggestive of a thriving commerce. Again, at the cemetery within the now torn and shattered Aurelian wall by the Porta San Paolo, they are often mowing of buttercups. "A light of laughing flowers along the grass is spread," says Shelley, whose child lies between Keats and the pyramid. But a couple of active scythes are kept at work there summer and spring--not that the grass is long, for it is much overtopped by the bee-orchis, but because flowers are not to laugh within reach of the civic vigilance.

Yet, except that it is overtaken and put to death in these accessible places, the wild summer growth of Rome has a prevailing success and victory. It breaks all bounds, flies to the summits, lodges in the sun, swings in the wind, takes wing to find the remotest ledges, and blooms

aloft. It makes light of the sixteenth century, of the seventeenth, and
of the eighteenth. As the historic ages grow cold it banters them alike.
The flagrant flourishing statue, the haughty facade, the broken pediment
(and Rome is chiefly the city of the broken pediment) are the
opportunities of this vagrant garden in the air. One certain church,
that is full of attitude, can hardly be aware that a crimson snapdragon
of great stature and many stalks and blossoms is standing on its furthest
summit tiptoe against its sky. The cornice of another church in the fair
middle of Rome lifts out of the shadows of the streets a row of
accidental marigolds. Impartial to the antique, the mediaeval, the
Renaissance early and late, the newer modern, this wild summer finds its
account in travertine and tufa, reticulated work, brick, stucco and
stone. "A bird of the air carries the matter," or the last sea-wind,
sombre and soft, or the latest tramontana, gold and blue, has lodged in a
little fertile dust the wild grass, wild wheat, wild oats!

If Venus had her runaway, after whom the Elizabethans raised hue and cry,
this is Ceres'. The municipal authorities, hot-foot, cannot catch it.
And, worse than all, if they pause, dismayed, to mark the flight of the
agile fugitive safe on the arc of a flying buttress, or taking the place
of the fallen mosaics and coloured tiles of a twelfth-century tower, and
in any case inaccessible, the grass grows under their discomfited feet.
It actually casts a flush of green over their city *piazza*--the wide
light-grey pavements so vast that to keep them weeded would need an army
of workers. That army has not been employed; and grass grows in a small
way, but still beautifully, in the wide space around which the tramway
circles. Perhaps a hatred of its delightful presence is what chiefly
prompts the civic government in Rome to the effort to turn the *piazza*
into a square. The shrub is to take the place not so much of the
pavement as of the importunate grass. For it is hard to be beaten--and
the weed does so prevail, is so small, and so dominant! The sun takes
its part, and one might almost imagine a sensitive Municipality in tears,
to see grass running, overhead and underfoot, through the "third" (which

is in truth the fourth) Rome.

When I say grass I use the word widely. Italian grass is not turf; it is full of things, and they are chiefly aromatic. No richer scents throng each other, close and warm, than these from a little hand-space of the grass one rests on, within the walls or on the plain, or in the Sabine or the Alban hills. Moreover, under the name I will take leave to include lettuce as it grows with a most welcome surprise on certain ledges of the Vatican. That great and beautiful palace is piled, at various angles, as it were house upon house, here magnificent, here careless, but with nothing pretentious and nothing furtive. And outside one lateral window on a ledge to the sun, prospers this little garden of random salad. Buckingham Palace has nothing whatever of the Vatican dignity, but one cannot well think of little cheerful cabbages sunning themselves on any parapet it may have round a corner.

Moreover, in Italy the vegetables--the table ones--have a wildness, a suggestion of the grass, from lands at liberty for all the tilling. Wildish peas, wilder asparagus--the field asparagus which seems to have disappeared from England, but of which Herrick boasts in his manifestations of frugality--and strawberries much less than half-way from the small and darkling ones of the woods to the pale and corpulent of the gardens, and with nothing of the wild fragrance lost--these are all Italian things of savage savour and simplicity. The most cultivated of all countries, the Italy of tillage, is yet not a garden, but something better, as her city is yet not a town but something better, and her wilderness something better than a desert. In all the three there is a trace of the little flying heels of the runaway.

A VANQUISHED MAN

Haydon died by his own act in 1846, and it was not, in the event, until 1853 that his journal was edited, not by Elizabeth Barrett Browning, as he wished, but by Tom Taylor. Turning over these familiar and famous volumes, often read, I wonder once more how any editor was bold to "take upon himself the mystery of things" in the case of Haydon, and to assign to that venial moral fault or this the ill-fortune and defeat that beset him, with hardly a pause for the renewal of the resistance of his admirable courage.

That he made a mere intellectual mistake, gave thanks with a lowly and lofty heart for a genius denied him, that he prepared himself to answer to Heaven and earth for the gift he had not, to suffer its reproach, to bear its burden, and that he looked for its reward, is all his history. There was no fault of the intellect in his apprehension of the thing he thought to stand possessed of. He conceived it aright, and he was just in his rebuke of a world so dull and trivial before the art for which he died. He esteemed it aright, except when he deemed it his.

His editor, thinking himself to be summoned to justify the chastisement, the destruction, the whole retribution of such a career, looks here and there for the sins of Haydon; the search is rewarded with the discovery of faults such as every man and woman entrusts to the common generosity, the general consciousness. It is a pity to see any man conning such offences by heart, and setting them clear in an editorial judgement because he thinks himself to hold a trust, by virtue of his biographical office, to explain the sufferings and the failure of a conquered man.

What, in the end, are the sins which are to lead the reader, sad but satisfied, to conclude with "See the result of--", or "So it ever must be

with him who yields to--," or whatever else may be the manner of
ratifying the sentence on the condemned and dead? Haydon, we hear,
omitted to ask advice, or, if he asked it, did not shape his course
thereby unless it pleased him. Haydon was self-willed; he had a wild
vanity, and he hoped he could persuade all the powers that include the
powers of man to prosper the work of which he himself was sure. He did
not wait upon the judgement of the world, but thought to compel it.

Should he, then, have waited upon the judgement of such a world? He was
foremost in the task of instructing, nay, of compelling it when there was
a question of the value of the Elgin Marbles, and when the
possession--which was the preservation--of these was at stake. There he
was not wrong; his judgement, that dealt him, in his own cause, the
first, the fatal, the final injury--the initial subtle blow that sent him
on his career so wronged, so cleft through and through, that the mere
course and action of life must ruin him--this judgement, in art, directed
him in the decision of the most momentous of all public questions. Haydon
admired, wrote, protested, declaimed, and fought; and in great part, it
seems, we owe our perpetual instruction by those judges of the Arts which
are the fragments of the Elgin sculptures, to the fact that Haydon
trusted himself with the trust that worked his own destruction. Into the
presence especially of those seated figures, commonly called the Fates,
we habitually bring our arts for sentence. He lent an effectual hand to
the setting-up of that Tribunal of headless stones.

The thing we should lament is rather that the world which refused,
neglected, forgot him--and by chance-medley was right, was right!--had no
possible authority for anything that it did against him, and that he
might have sent it to school, for all his defect of genius; moreover,
that he was mortally wounded in the last of his forty years of battle by
this ironic wound: among the bad painters chosen to adorn the Houses of
Parliament with fresco, he was not one. This affront he took at the
hands of men who had no real distinctions in their gift. He might well

have had, by mere chance, some great companion with whom to share that rejection. The unfortunate man had no such fortuitous fellowship at hand. How strange, the solitude of the bad painter outcast by the worst, and capable of making common cause indomitably with the good, had there been any such to take heart from his high courage!

There was none. There were ranged the unjust judges with their blunders all in good order, and their ignorance new dressed, and there was no artist to destroy except only this one, somewhat better than their favoured, their appointed painters in fresco; one uncompanioned, and a man besides through whose heart the public reproach was able to cut keenly.

Is this sensibility to be made a reproach to Haydon? It has always seemed to me that he was not without greatness--yet he was always without dignity--in those most cruel passages of his life, such as that of his defeat, towards the close of his war, by the show of a dwarf, to which all London thronged, led by Royal example, while the exhibition of his picture was deserted. He was not betrayed by anger at this end of hopes and labours in which all that a man lives for had been pledged. Nay, he succeeded in bearing what a more inward man would have taken more hardly. He was able to say in his loud voice, in reproach to the world, what another would have barred within: one of his great pictures was in a cellar, another in an attic, another at the pawnbroker's, another in a grocer's shop, another unfinished in his studio; the bills for frames and colours and the rent were unpaid. Some solace he even found in stating a few of these facts, in French, to a French official or diplomatic visitor to London, interested in the condition of the arts. Well, who shall live without support? A man finds it where he can.

After these offences of self-will and vanity Tom Taylor finds us some other little thing--I think it is inaccuracy. Poor Haydon says in one phrase that he paid all his friends on such a day, and in another soon following that the money given or lent to him had been insufficient to pay them completely; and assuredly there are many revisions, after-thoughts, or other accidents to account for such a slip. His editor says the discrepancy is "characteristic," but I protest I cannot find another like it among those melancholy pages. If something graver could but be sifted out from all these journals and letters of frank confession, by the explainer! Here, then, is the last and least: Haydon was servile in his address to "men of rank." But his servility seems to be very much in the fashion of his day--nothing grosser; and the men who set the fashion had not to shape their style to Haydon's perpetual purpose, which was to ask for commissions or for money.

Not the forsaken man only but also the fallen city evokes this exercise of historical morality, until a man in flourishing London is not afraid to assign the causes of the decay of Venice; and there is not a watering place upon our coasts but is securely aware of merited misfortune on the Adriatic.

Haydon was grateful, and he helped men in trouble; he had pupils, and never a shilling in pay for teaching them. He painted a good thing--the head of his Lazarus. He had no fault of theory: what fault of theory can a man commit who stands, as he did, by "Nature and the Greeks"? In theory he soon outgrew the Italians then most admired; he had an honest mind.

But nothing was able to gain for him the pardon that is never to be gained, the impossible pardon--pardon for that first and last mistake--the mistake as to his own powers. If to pardon means to dispense from consequence, how should this be pardoned? Art would cease to be itself, by such an amnesty.

A NORTHERN FANCY

"I remember," said Dryden, writing to Dennis, "I remember poor Nat Lee, who was then upon the verge of madness, yet made a sober and witty answer to a bad poet who told him, 'It was an easy thing to write like a madman.' 'No,' said he, ''tis a very difficult thing to write like a madman, but 'tis a very easy thing to write like a fool.'" Nevertheless, the difficult song of distraction is to be heard, a light high note, in English poetry throughout two centuries at least, and one English poet lately set that untethered lyric, the mad maid's song, flying again.

A revolt against the oppression of the late sixteenth and early seventeenth centuries--the age of the re-discovery of death; against the crime of tragedies; against the tyranny of Italian example that had made the poets walk in one way of love, scorn, constancy, inconstancy--may have caused this trolling of unconsciousness, this tune of innocence, and this carol of liberty, to be held so dear. "I heard a maid in Bedlam," runs the old song. High and low the poets tried for that note, and the singer was nearly always to be a maid and crazed for love. Except for the temporary insanity so indifferently worn by the soprano of the now deceased kind of Italian opera, and except that a recent French story plays with the flitting figure of a village girl robbed of her wits by woe (and this, too, is a Russian villager, and the Southern author may have found his story on the spot, as he seems to aver) I have not met elsewhere than in England this solitary and detached poetry of the treble note astray.

At least, it is principally a northern fancy. Would the steadfast Cordelia, if she had not died, have lifted the low voice to that high note, so delicately untuned? She who would not be prodigal of words might yet, indeed, have sung in the cage, and told old tales, and laughed at gilded butterflies of the court of crimes, and lived so long in the strange health of an emancipated brain as to wear out

> Packs and sects of great ones
> That ebb and flow by the moon.

She, if King Lear had had his last desire, might have sung the merry and strange tune of Bedlam, like the slighter Ophelia and the maid called Barbara.

It was surely the name of the maid who died singing, as Desdemona remembers, that lingered in the ear of Wordsworth. Of all the songs of the distracted, written in the sanity of high imagination, there is nothing more passionate than that beginning "'Tis said that some have died for love." To one who has always recognized the greatness of this poem and who possibly had known and forgotten how much Ruskin prized it, it was a pleasure to find the judgement afresh in ***Modern Painters***, where this grave lyric is cited for an example of great imagination. It is the mourning and restless song of the lover ("the pretty Barbara died") who has not yet broken free from memory into the alien world of the insane.

Barbara's lover dwelt in the scene of his love, as Dryden's Adam entreats the expelling angel that he might do, protesting that he could endure to lose "the bliss, but not the place." (And although this dramatic "Paradise Lost" of Dryden's is hardly named by critics except to be scorned, this is assuredly a fine and imaginative thought.) It is nevertheless as a wanderer that the crazed creature visits the fancy of English poets with such a wild recurrence. The Englishman of the far past, barred by climate, bad roads, ill-lighted winters, and the intricate life and customs of the little town, must have been generally a home-keeper. No adventure, no setting forth, and small liberty, for him. But Tom-a-Bedlam, the wild man in patches or in ribbons, with his wallet and his horn for alms of food or drink, came and went as fitfully as the storm, free to suffer all the cold--an unsheltered creature; and the chill fancy of the villager followed him out to the heath on a journey that had no law. Was it he in person, or a poet for him, that made the swinging song: "From the hag and the hungry goblin"? If a poet, it was one who wrote like a madman and not like a fool.

Not a town, not a village, not a solitary cottage during the English Middle Ages was unvisited by him who frightened the children; they had a name for him as for the wild birds--Robin Redbreast, Dicky Swallow, Philip Sparrow, Tom Tit, Tom-a-Bedlam. And after him came the "Abram men," who were sane parodies of the crazed, and went to the fairs and wakes in motley. Evelyn says of a fop: "All his body was dressed like a maypole, or a Tom-a-Bedlam's cap." But after the Civil Wars they vanished, and no man knew how. In time old men remembered them only to remember that they had not seen any such companies or solitary wanderers of late years.

The mad maid of the poets is a vagrant too, when she is free, and not singing within Bedlam early in the morning, "in the spring." Wordsworth, who dealt with the legendary fancy in his "Ruth," makes the crazed one a wanderer in the hills whom a traveller might see by chance, rare as an Oread, and nearly as wild as Echo herself:-

> I too have passed her in the hills
> Setting her little water-mills.

His heart misgives him to think of the rheumatism that must befall in such a way of living; and his grave sense of civilization, **bourgeois** in the humane and noble way that is his own, restores her after death to the company of man, to the "holy bell," which Shakespeare's Duke remembered in banishment, and to the congregation and their "Christian psalm."

The older poets were less responsible, less serious and more sad, than Wordsworth, when they in turn were touched by the fancy of the maid crazed by love. They left her to her light immortality; and she might be drenched in dews; they would not desire to reconcile nor bury her. She might have her hair torn by the bramble, but her heart was light after trouble. "Many light hearts and wings"--she had at least the bird's heart, and the poet lent to her voice the wings of his verses.

There is nothing in our poetry less modern than she. The vagrant woman of later feeling was rather the sane creature of Ebenezer Elliott's fine lines in "The Excursion"--

  Bone-weary, many-childed, trouble-tried!
  Wife of my bosom, wedded to my soul!

Trouble did not "try" the Elizabethan wild one, it undid her. She had no child, or if there had ever been a child of hers, she had long forgotten how it died. She hailed the wayfarer, who was more weary than she, with a song; she haunted the cheerful dawn; her "good-morrow" rings from Herrick's poem, fresh as cock-crow. She knows that her love is dead, and her perplexity has regard rather to the many kinds of flowers than to the old story of his death; they distract her in the splendid meadows.

All the tragic world paused to hear that lightest of songs, as the tragedy of Hamlet pauses for the fitful voice of Ophelia. Strange was the charm of this perpetual alien, and unknown to us now. The world has become once again as it was in the mad maid's heyday, less serious and more sad than Wordsworth; but it has not recovered, and perhaps will never recover, that sweetness. Blake's was a more starry madness. Crabbe, writing of village sorrows, thought himself bound to recur to the legend of the mad maid, but his "crazed maiden" is sane enough, sorrowful but dull, and sings of her own "burning brow," as Herrick's wild one never sang; nor is there any smile in her story, though she talks of flowers, or, rather, "the herbs I loved to rear"; and perhaps she is the surest of all signs that the strange inspiration of the past centuries was lost, vanished like Tom-a-Bedlam himself. It had been wholly English, whereas the English eighteenth century was not wholly English.

It is not to be imagined that any hard Southern mind could ever have played in poetry with such a fancy; or that Petrarch, for example, could so have foregone the manifestation of intelligence and intelligible sentiment. And as to Dante, who put the two eternities into the momentary balance of the human will, cold would be his disregard of this northern dream of innocence. If the mad maid was an alien upon earth, what were she in the Inferno? What word can express her strangeness there, her vagrancy there? And with what eyes would they see this dewy face glancing in at the windows of that City?

LAUGHTER

Times have been, it is said, merrier than these; but it is certain nevertheless that laughter never was so honoured as now; were it not for the paradox one might say, it never was so grave. Everywhere the joke "emerges"--as an "elegant" writer might have it--emerges to catch the attention of the sense of humour; and everywhere the sense of humour wanders, watches, and waits to honour the appeal.

It loiters, vaguely but perpetually willing. It wears (let the violent personification be pardoned) a hanging lip, and a wrinkle in abeyance, and an eye in suspense. It is much at the service of the vagrant encounterer, and may be accosted by any chance daughters of the game. It stands in untoward places, or places that were once inappropriate, and is early at some indefinite appointment, some ubiquitous tryst, with the compliant jest.

All literature becomes a field of easy assignations; there is a constant signalling, an endless recognition. Forms of approach are remitted. And the joke and the sense of humour, with no surprise of meeting, or no gaiety of strangeness, so customary has the promiscuity become, go up and down the pages of the paper and the book. See, again, the theatre. A somewhat easy sort of comic acting is by so much the best thing upon our present stage that little else can claim--paradox again apart--to be taken seriously.

There is, in a word, a determination, an increasing tendency away from the Oriental estimate of laughter as a thing fitter for women, fittest for children, and unfitted for the beard. Laughter is everywhere and at every moment proclaimed to be the honourable occupation of men, and in some degree distinctive of men, and no mean part of their prerogative and privilege. The sense of humour is chiefly theirs, and those who are not men are to be admitted to the jest upon their explanation. They will not refuse explanation. And there is little upon which a man will so value himself as upon that sense, "in England, now."

Meanwhile, it would be a pity if laughter should ever become, like rhetoric and the arts, a habit. And it is in some sort a habit when it is not inevitable. If we ask ourselves why we laugh, we must confess that we laugh oftenest because--being amused--we intend to show that we are amused. We are right to make the sign, but a smile would be as sure a signal as a laugh, and more sincere; it would but be changing the convention; and the change would restore laughter itself to its own place. We have fallen into the way of using it to prove something--our sense of the goodness of the jest, to wit; but laughter should not thus be used, it should go free. It is not a demonstration, whether in logic, or--as the word demonstration is now generally used--in emotion; and we do ill to charge it with that office.

Something of the Oriental idea of dignity might not be amiss among such a people as ourselves containing wide and numerous classes who laugh without cause: audiences; crowds; a great many clergymen, who perhaps first fell into the habit in the intention of proving that they were not gloomy; but a vast number of laymen also who had not that excuse; and many women who laugh in their uncertainty as to what is humorous and what is not. This last is the most harmless of all kinds of superfluous laughter. When it carries an apology, a confession of natural and genial ignorance, and when a gentle creature laughs a laugh of hazard and experiment, she is to be more than forgiven. What she must not do is to laugh a laugh of instruction, and as it were retrieve the jest that was never worth the taking.

There are, besides, a few women who do not disturb themselves as to a sense of humour, but who laugh from a sense of happiness. Childish is that trick, and sweet. For children, who always laugh because they must, and never by way of proof or sign, laugh only half their laughs out of their sense of humour; they laugh the rest under a mere stimulation: because of abounding breath and blood; because some one runs behind them, for example, and movement does so jog their spirits that their legs fail them, for laughter, without a jest.

If ever the day should come when men and women shall be content to signal their perception of humour by the natural smile, and shall keep the laugh for its own unpremeditated act, shall laugh seldom, and simply, and not thrice at the same thing--once for foolish surprise, and twice for tardy intelligence, and thrice to let it be known that they are amused--then it may be time to persuade this laughing nation not to laugh so loud as it is wont in public. The theatre audiences of louder-speaking nations laugh lower than ours. The laugh that is chiefly a signal of the laugher's sense of the ridiculous is necessarily loud; and it has the disadvantage of covering what we may perhaps wish to hear from the actors. It is a public laugh, and no ordinary citizen is called upon for a public laugh. He may laugh in public, but let it be with private laughter there.

Let us, if anything like a general reform be possible in these times of dispersion and of scattering, keep henceforth our sense of humour in a place better guarded, as something worth a measure of seclusion. It should not loiter in wait for the alms of a joke in adventurous places. For the sense of humour has other things to do than to make itself conspicuous in the act of laughter. It has negative tasks of valid virtue; for example, the standing and waiting within call of tragedy itself, where, excluded, it may keep guard.

No reasonable man will aver that the Oriental manners are best. This would be to deny Shakespeare as his comrades knew him, where the wit "out-did the meat, out-did the frolic wine," and to deny Ben Jonson's "tart Aristophanes, neat Terence, witty Plautus," and the rest. Doubtless Greece determined the custom for all our Occident; but none the less might the modern world grow more sensible of the value of composure.

To none other of the several powers of our souls do we so give rein as to this of humour, and none other do we indulge with so little fastidiousness. It is as though there were honour in governing the other senses, and honour in refusing to govern this. It is as though we were ashamed of reason here, and shy of dignity, and suspicious of temperance, and diffident of moderation, and too eager to thrust forward that which loses nothing by seclusion.

HARLEQUIN MERCUTIO

The first time that Mercutio fell upon the English stage, there fell with him a gay and hardly human figure; it fell, perhaps finally, for English drama. That manner of man--Arlecchino, or Harlequin--had outlived his playmates, Pantaleone, Brighella, Colombina, and the Clown. A little of Pantaleone survives in old Capulet, a little in the father of the Shrew, but the life of Mercutio in the one play, and of the subordinate Tranio in the other, is less quickly spent, less easily put out, than the smouldering of the old man. Arlecchino frolics in and out of the tragedy and comedy of Shakespeare, until he thus dies in his lightest, his brightest, his most vital shape.

Arlecchino, the tricksy and shifty spirit, the contriver, the busybody, the trusty rogue, the wonder-worker, the man in disguise, the mercurial one, lives on buoyantly in France to the age of Moliere. He is officious and efficacious in the skin of Mascarille and Ergaste and Scapin; but he tends to be a lacquey, with a reference rather to Antiquity and the Latin comedy than to the Middle Ages, as on the English stage his mere memory survives differently to a later age in the person of "Charles, his friend." What convinces me that he virtually died with Mercutio is chiefly this--that this comrade of Romeo's lives so keenly as to be fully capable of the death that he takes at Tybalt's sword-point; he lived indeed, he dies indeed. Another thing that marks the close of a career of ages is his loss of his long customary good luck. Who ever heard of Arlecchino unfortunate before, at fault with his sword-play, overtaken by tragedy? His time had surely come. The gay companion was to bleed; Tybalt's sword had made a way. 'Twas not so deep as a well nor so wide as a church-door, but it served.

Some confusion comes to pass among the typical figures of the primitive

Italian play, because Harlequin, on that conventional little stage of the past, has a hero's place, whereas when he interferes in human affairs he is only the auxiliary. He might be lover and bridegroom on the primitive stage, in the comedy of these few and unaltered types; but when Pantaloon, Clown, and Harlequin play with really human beings, then Harlequin can be no more than a friend of the hero, the friend of the bridegroom. The five figures of the old stage dance attendance; they play around the business of those who have the dignity of mortality; they, poor immortals--a clown who does not die, a pantaloon never far from death, who yet does not die, a Columbine who never attains Desdemona's death of innocence or Juliet's death of rectitude and passion--flit in the backward places of the stage.

Ariel fulfils his office, and is not of one kind with those he serves. Is there a memory of Harlequin in that delicate figure? Something of the subservient immortality, of the light indignity, proper to Pantaleone, Brighella, Arlecchino, Colombina, and the Clown, hovers away from the stage when Ariel is released from the trouble of human things.

Immortality, did I say? It was immortality until Mercutio fell. And if some claim be made to it still because Harlequin has transformed so many scenes for the pleasure of so many thousand children, since Mercutio died, I must reply that our modern Harlequin is no more than a *__marionnette__*; he has returned whence he came. A man may play him, but he is--as he was first of all--a doll. From doll-hood Arlecchino took life, and, so promoted, flitted through a thousand comedies, only to be again what he first was; save that, as once a doll played the man, so now a man plays the doll. It is but a memory of Arlecchino that our children see, a poor statue or image endowed with mobility rather than with life.

With Mercutio, vanished the light heart that had given to the serious ages of the world an hour's refuge from the unforgotten burden of responsible conscience; the light heart assumed, borrowed, made dramatically the spectator's own. We are not serious now, and no heart now is quite light, even for an hour.

THE LITTLE LANGUAGE

Dialect is the elf rather than the genius of place, and a dwarfish master of the magic of local things.

In England we hardly know what a concentrated homeliness it nourishes; inasmuch as, with us, the castes and classes for whom Goldoni and Gallina and Signor Fogazzaro have written in the patois of the Veneto, use no dialect at all.

Neither Goldoni nor Gallina has charged the Venetian language with so much literature as to take from the people the shelter of their almost unwritten tongue. Signor Fogazzaro, bringing tragedy into the homes of dialect, does but show us how the language staggers under such a stress, how it breaks down, and resigns that office. One of the finest of the characters in the ranks of his admirable fiction is that old manageress of the narrow things of the house whose daughter is dying insane. I have called the dialect a shelter. This it is; but the poor lady does not cower within; her resigned head erect, she is shut out from that homely refuge, suffering and inarticulate. The two dramatists in their several centuries also recognized the inability of the dialect. They laid none but light loads upon it. They caused it to carry no more in their homely plays than it carries in homely life. Their work leaves it what it was--the talk of a people talking much about few things; a people like our own and any other in their lack of literature, but local and all Italian in their lack of silence.

Common speech is surely a greater part of life to such a people than to one less pleased with chatter or more pleased with books. I am writing of men, women, and children (and children are not forgotten, since we share a patois with children on terms of more than common equality) who possess, for all occasions of ceremony and opportunities of dignity, a general, national, liberal, able, and illustrious tongue, charged with all its history and all its achievements; for the speakers of dialect, of a certain rank, speak Italian, too. But to tamper with their dialect, or to take it from them, would be to leave them houseless and exposed in their daily business. So much does their patois seem to be their refuge from the heavy and multitudinous experiences of a literary tongue, that the stopping of a fox's earth might be taken as the image of any act that should spoil or stop the talk of the associated seclusion of their town, and leave them in the bleakness of a larger patriotism.

The Venetian people, the Genoese, and the other speakers of languages that might all have proved right "Italian" had not Dante, Petrarch and Boccaccio written in Tuscan, can neither write nor be taught hard things in their dialect, although they can live, whether easy lives or hard, and evidently can die, therein. The hands and feet that have served the villager and the citizen at homely tasks have all the lowliness of his patois, to his mind; and when he must perforce yield up their employment, we may believe that it is a simple thing to die in so simple and so narrow a language, one so comfortable, neighbourly, tolerant, and compassionate; so confidential; so incapable, ignorant, unappalling, inapt to wing any wearied thought upon difficult flight or to spur it upon hard travelling.

Not without words is mental pain, or even physical pain, to be undergone; but the words that have done no more than order the things of the narrow street are not words to put a fine edge or a piercing point to any human pang. It may even well be that to die in dialect is easier than to die in the eloquence of Manfred, though that declaimed language, too, is doubtless a defence, if one of a different manner.

These writers in Venetian--they are named because in no other Italian dialect has work so popular as Goldoni's been done, nor so excellent as Signor Fogazzaro's--have left the unlettered local language in which they loved to deal, to its proper limitations. They have not given weighty things into its charge, nor made it heavily responsible. They have added nothing to it; nay, by writing it they might even be said to have made it duller, had it not been for the reader and the actor. Insomuch as the intense expressiveness of a dialect--of a small vocabulary in the mouth of a dramatic people--lies in the various accent wherewith a southern citizen knows how to enrich his talk, it remains for the actor to restore its life to the written phrase. In dialect the author is forbidden to search for the word, for there is none lurking for his choice; but of tones, allusions, and of references and inferences of the voice, the speaker of dialect is a master. No range of phrases can be his, but he has the more or the less confidential inflection, until at times the close communication of the narrow street becomes a very conspiracy.

Let it be borne in mind that dialect properly so called is something all unlike, for instance, the mere jargon of London streets. The difference may be measured by the fact that Italian dialects have a highly organized and orderly grammar. The Londoner cannot keep the small and loose order of the grammar of good English; the Genoese conjugates his patois verbs, with subjunctives and all things of that handsome kind, lacked by the English of Universities.

The middle class--the *piccolo mondo*--hat shares Italian dialect with the poor are more strictly local in their manners than either the opulent or the indigent of the same city. They have moreover the busy intelligence (which is the intellect of patois) at its keenest. Their speech keeps them a sequestered place which is Italian, Italian beyond the ken of the traveller, and beyond the reach of alteration. And--what is pretty to observe--the speakers are well conscious of the characters of this intimate language. An Italian countryman who has known no other climate will vaunt, in fervent platitudes, his Italian sun; in like manner he is conscious of the local character of his language, and tucks himself within it at home, whatever Tuscan he may speak abroad. A properly spelt letter, Swift said, would seem to expose him and Mrs Dingley and Stella to the eyes of the world; but their little language, ill-written, was "snug."

Lovers have made a little language in all times; finding the nobler language insufficient, do they ensconce themselves in the smaller? discard noble and literary speech as not noble enough, and in despair thus prattle and gibber and stammer? Rather perhaps this departure from English is but an excursion after gaiety. The ideal lovers, no doubt, would be so simple as to be grave. That is a tenable opinion. Nevertheless, age by age they have been gay; and age by age they have exchanged language imitated from the children they doubtless never studied, and perhaps never loved. Why so? They might have chosen broken English of other sorts--that, for example, which was once thought amusing in farce, as spoken by the Frenchman conceived by the Englishman--a complication of humour fictitious enough, one might think, to please anyone; or else a fragment of negro dialect; or the style of telegrams; or the masterly adaptation of the simple savage's English devised by Mrs Plornish in her intercourse with the Italian. But none of these found favour. The choice has always been of the language of children. Let us suppose that the flock of winged Loves worshipping Venus in the Titian picture, and the noble child that rides his lion erect with a background of Venetian gloomy dusk, may be the inspirers of those prattlings. "See then thy selfe likewise art lyttle made," says Spenser's Venus to her child.

Swift was the best prattler. He had caught the language, surprised it in

Stella when she was veritably a child. He did not push her clumsily back into a childhood he had not known; he simply prolonged in her a childhood he had loved. He is "seepy." "Nite, dealest dea, nite dealest logue." It is a real good-night. It breathes tenderness from that moody and uneasy bed of projects.

ANIMA PELLEGRINA!

Every language in the world has its own phrase, fresh for the stranger's fresh and alien sense of its signal significance; a phrase that is its own essential possession, and yet is dearer to the speaker of other tongues. Easily--shall I say cheaply?--spiritual, for example, was the nation that devised the name *anima pellegrina*, wherewith to crown a creature admired. "Pilgrim soul" is a phrase for any language, but "pilgrim soul!" addressed, singly and sweetly to one who cannot be over-praised, "pilgrim-soul!" is a phrase of fondness, the high homage of a lover, of one watching, of one who has no more need of common flatteries, but has admired and gazed while the object of his praises visibly surpassed them--this is the facile Italian ecstasy, and it rises into an Italian heaven.

It was by chance, and in an old play, that I came upon this impetuous, sudden, and single sentence of admiration, as it were a sentence of life passed upon one charged with inestimable deeds; and the modern editor had thought it necessary to explain the exclamation by a note. It was, he said, poetical.

Anima pellegrina seems to be Italian of no later date than Pergolese's airs, and suits the time as the familiar phrase of the more modern love-song suited the day of Bellini. But it is only Italian, bygone Italian, and not a part of the sweet past of any other European nation, but only of this.

To the same local boundaries and enclosed skies belongs the charm of those buoyant words:-

Felice chi vi mira,
Ma piu felice chi per voi sospira!

And it is not only a charm of elastic sound or of grace; that would be but a property of the turn of speech. It is rather the profounder advantage whereby the rhymes are freighted with such feeling as the very language keeps in store. In another tongue you may sing, "happy who looks, happier who sighs"; but in what other tongue shall the little meaning be so sufficient, and in what other shall you get from so weak an antithesis the illusion of a lovely intellectual epigram? Yet it is not worthy of an English reader to call it an illusion; he should rather be glad to travel into the place of a language where the phrase *is* intellectual, impassioned, and an epigram; and should thankfully for the occasion translate himself, and not the poetry.

I have been delighted to use a present current phrase whereof the charm may still be unknown to Englishmen--"*piuttosto bruttini*." See what an all-Italian spirit is here, and what contempt, not reluctant, but tolerant and familiar. You may hear it said of pictures, or works of art of several kinds, and you confess at once that not otherwise should they be condemned. **Brutto**--ugly--is the word of justice, the word for any language, everywhere translatable, a circular note, to be exchanged internationally with a general meaning, wholesale, in the course of the European concert. But **bruttino** is a soothing diminutive, a diminutive that forbears to express contempt, a diminutive that implies innocence, and is, moreover, guarded by a hesitating adverb, shrugging in the rear--"rather than not." "Rather ugly than not, and ugly in a little way that we need say few words about--the fewer the better;" nay, this paraphrase cannot achieve the homely Italian quality whereby the printed and condemnatory criticism is made a family affair that shall go no further. After the sound of it, the European concert seems to be composed of brass instruments.

How unlike is the house of English language and the enclosure into which a traveller hither has to enter! Do we possess anything here more essentially ours (though we share it with our sister Germany) than our particle "un"? Poor are those living languages that have not our use of so rich a negative. The French equivalent in adjectives reaches no further than the adjective itself--or hardly; it does not attain the participle; so that no French or Italian poet has the words "unloved", "unforgiven." None such, therefore, has the opportunity of the gravest and the most majestic of all ironies. In our English, the words that are denied are still there--"loved," "forgiven": excluded angels, who stand erect, attesting what is not done, what is undone, what shall not be done.

No merely opposite words could have so much denial, or so much pain of loss, or so much outer darkness, or so much barred beatitude in sight. All-present, all-significant, all-remembering, all-foretelling is the word, and it has a plenitude of knowledge.

We have many more conspicuous possessions that are, like this, proper to character and thought, and by no means only an accident of untransferable speech. And it is impossible for a reader, who is a lover of languages for their spirit, to pass the words of untravelled excellence, proper to their own garden enclosed, without recognition. Never may they be disregarded or confounded with the universal stock. If I would not so neglect *piuttosto bruttini*, how much less a word dominating literature! And of such words of ascendancy and race there is no great

English author but has abundant possession. No need to recall them. But even writers who are not great have, here and there, proved their full consciousness of their birthright. Thus does a man who was hardly an author, Haydon the painter, put out his hand to take his rights. He has incomparable language when he is at a certain page of his life; at that time he sate down to sketch his child, dying in its babyhood, and the head he studied was, he says, full of "power and grief."

This is a phrase of different discovery from that which reveals a local rhyme-balanced epigram, a gracious antithesis, taking an intellectual place--***Felice chi vi mira***--or the art-critic's phrase--piuttosto bruttini--of easy, companionable, and equal contempt.

As for French, if it had no other sacred words--and it has many--who would not treasure the language that has given us--no, not that has given us, but that has kept for its own--***ensoleillé***? Nowhere else is the sun served with such a word. It is not to be said or written without a convincing sense of sunshine, and from the very word come light and radiation. The unaccustomed north could not have made it, nor the accustomed south, but only a nation part-north and part-south; therefore neither England nor Italy can rival it. But there needed also the senses of the French--those senses of which they say far too much in every second-class book of their enormous, their general second-class, but which they have matched in their time with some inimitable words. Perhaps that matching was done at the moment of the full literary consciousness of the senses, somewhere about the famous 1830. For I do not think *ensoleillé* to be a much older word--I make no assertion. Whatever its origin, may it have no end! They cannot weary us with it; for it seems as new as the sun, as remote as old Provence; village, hill-side, vineyard, and chestnut wood shine in the splendour of the word, the air is light, and white things passing blind the eyes--a woman's linen, white cattle, shining on the way from shadow to shadow. A word of the sense of sight, and a summer word, in short, compared with which the paraphrase is but a picture. For ***ensoleille*** I would claim the consent of all readers--that they shall all acknowledge the spirit of that French. But perhaps it is a mere personal preference that makes le jour s'annonce also sacred.

If the hymn, "Stabat Mater dolorosa," was written in Latin, this could be only that it might in time find its true language and incomparable phrase at last--that it might await the day of life in its proper German. I found it there (and knew at once the authentic verse, and knew at once for what tongue it had been really destined) in the pages of the prayer-book of an apple-woman at an Innsbruck church, and in the accents of her voice.

THE SEA WALL

A singular love of walls is mine. Perhaps because of childish association with mountain-climbing roads narrow in the bright shadows of grey stone, hiding olive trees whereof the topmost leaves prick above into the blue; or perhaps because of subsequent living in London, with its too many windows and too few walls, the city which of all capitals takes least visible hold upon the ground; or for the sake of some other attraction or aversion, walls, blank and strong, reaching outward at the base, are a satisfaction to the eyes teased by the inexpressive peering of windows, by that weak lapse and shuffling which is the London "area," and by the helpless hollows of shop-fronts.

I would rather have a wall than any rail but a very good one of wrought-iron. A wall is the safeguard of simplicity. It lays a long level line among the indefinite chances of the landscape. But never more majestic than in face of the wild sea, the wall, steadying its slanting foot upon the rock, builds in the serried ilex-wood and builds out the wave. The sea-wall is the wall at its best. And fine as it is on the strong coast, it is beautiful on the weak littoral and the imperilled levels of a northern beach.

That sea wall is low and long; sea-pinks grow on the salt grass that passes away into shingle at its foot. It is at close quarters with the winter sea, when, from the low coast with its low horizon, the sky-line of sea is jagged. Never from any height does the ocean-horizon show thus broken and battered at its very verge, but from the flat coast and the narrow world you can see the wave as far as you can see the water; and the stormy light of a clear horizon is seen to be mobile and shifting with the buoyant hillocks and their restless line.

Nowhere in Holland does there seem to be such a low sea-wall as secures many a mile of gentle English coast to the east. The Dutch dyke has not that aspect of a lowly parapet against a tide; it springs with a look of haste and of height; and when you first run upstairs from the encumbered Dutch fields to look at the sea, there is nothing in the least like England; and even the Englishman of to-day is apt to share something of the old perversity that was minded to cast derision upon the Dutch in their encounters with the tides.

There has been some fault in the Dutch, making them subject to the slight derision of the nations who hold themselves to be more romantic, and, as it were, more slender. We English, once upon a time, did especially flout the little nation then acting a history that proved worth the writing. It may be no more than a brief perversity that has set a number of our writers to cheer the memory of Charles II. Perhaps, even, it is no more than another rehearsal of that untiring success at the expense of the bourgeois. The bourgeois would be more simple than, in fact, he is were he to stand up every time to be shocked; but, perhaps, the image of his dismay is enough to reward the fancy of those who practise the wanton art. And, when all is done, who performs for any but an imaginary audience? Surely those companies of spectators and of auditors are not the least of the makings of an author. A few men and women he achieves within his books; but others does he create without, and to those figures of all illusion makes the appeal of his art. More candid is the author who has no world, but turns that appeal inwards to his own heart. He has at least a living hearer.

This is by the way. Charles II has been cheered; the feat is done, the dismay is imagined with joy. And yet the Merry Monarch's was a dismal time. Plague, fire, the arrears of pension from the French King remembered and claimed by the restored throne of England, and the Dutch in the Medway--all this was disaster. None the less, having the vanity of new clothes and a pretty figure, did we--especially by the mouth of Andrew Marvell--deride our victors, making sport of the Philistines with a proper national sense of enjoyment of such physical disabilities, or such natural difficulties, or such misfavour of fortune, as may beset the alien.

Especially were the denials of fortune matter for merriment. They are so still; or they were so certainly in the day when a great novelist found the smallness of some South German States to be the subject of unsating banter. The German scenes at the end of "Vanity Fair," for example, may prove how much the ridicule of mere smallness, fewness, poverty (and not even real poverty, privation, but the poverty that shows in comparison with the gold of great States, and is properly in proportion) rejoiced the sense of humour in a writer and moralist who intended to teach mankind to be less worldly. In Andrew Marvell's day they were even more candid. The poverty of privation itself was provocative of the sincere laughter of the inmost man, the true, infrequent laughter of the heart. Marvell, the Puritan, laughed that very laughter--at leanness, at hunger, cold, and solitude--in the face of the world, and in the name of literature, in one memorable satire. I speak of "Flecno, an English Priest in Rome," wherein nothing is spared--not the smallness of the lodging, nor the lack of a bed, nor the scantiness of clothing, nor the fast.

"This basso-rilievo of a man--"

personal meagreness is the first joke and the last.

It is not to be wondered at that he should find in the smallness of the country of Holland matter for a cordial jest. But, besides the smallness, there was that accidental and natural disadvantage in regard to the sea. In the Venetians, commerce with the sea, conflict with the sea, a victory over the sea, and the ensuing peace--albeit a less instant battle and a more languid victory--were confessed to be noble; in the Dutch they were grotesque. "With mad labour," says Andrew Marvell, with the spirited consciousness of the citizen of a country well above ground and free to watch the labour at leisure, "with mad labour" did the Dutch "fish the land to shore."

> How did they rivet with gigantic piles,
> Thorough the centre, their new-catched miles,
> And to the stake a struggling country bound,
> Where barking waves still bait the forced ground;
> Building their watery Babel far more high
> To reach the sea than those to scale the sky!

It is done with a jolly wit, and in what admirable couplets!

> The fish oft-times the burgher dispossessed,
> And sat, not as a meat, but as a guest.

And it is even better sport that the astonished tritons and sea-nymphs should find themselves provided with a capital ***cabillau*** of shoals of pickled Dutchmen (heeren for herring, says Marvell); and it must be allowed that he rhymes with the enjoyment of irony. There is not a smile for us in "Flecno," but it is more than possible to smile over this "Character of Holland"; at the excluded ocean returning to play at leap-frog over the steeples; at the rise of government and authority in Holland, which belonged of right to the man who could best invent a shovel or a pump, the country being so leaky:-

> Not who first sees the rising sun commands,
> But who could first discern the rising lands.

We have lost something more than the delighted laughter of Marvell, more than his practical joke, and more than the heart that was light in so burly a frame--we have lost with these the wild humour that wore so well the bonds of two equal lines, and was wild with so much order, invention, malice, gaiety, polish, equilibrium, and vitality--in a word, the Couplet, the couplet of the past. We who cannot stand firm within two lines, but must slip beyond and between the boundaries, who tolerate the couplets of Keats and imitate them, should praise the day of Charles II because of Marvell's art, and not for love of the sorry reign. We had plague, fire, and the Dutch in the Medway, but we had the couplet; and there were also the measures of those more poetic poets, hitherto called somewhat slightingly the Cavalier poets, who matched the wit of the Puritan with a spirit simpler and less mocking.

It was against an English fortress, profoundly walled, that some remembered winter storms lately turned their great artillery. It was a time of resounding nights; the sky was so clamorous and so close, up in the towers of the seaside stronghold, that one seemed to be indeed admitted to the perturbed counsels of the winds. The gale came with an indescribable haste, hooting as it flew; it seemed to break itself upon the heights, yet passed unbroken out to sea; in the voice of the sea there were pauses, but none in that of the urgent gale with its hoo-hoo-hoo all night, that clamoured down the calling of the waves. That lack of pauses was the strangest thing in the tempest, because the increase of sound seemed to imply a lull before. The lull was never perceptible, but the lift was always an alarm. The onslaught was instant, where would it stop? What was the secret extreme to which this hurry and force were tending? You asked less what thing was driving the flocks of the storm than what was drawing them. The attraction seemed the greater violence, the more irresistible, and the more unknown. And there were moments when the end seemed about to be attained.

The wind struck us hasty blows, and unawares we borrowed, to describe it, words fit for the sharp strokes of material things; but the fierce gale is soft. Along the short grass, trembling and cowering flat on the scarped hill-side, against the staggering horse, against the flint walls, one with the rock they grasp, the battery of the tempest is a quick and enormous softness. What down, what sand, what deep moss, what elastic wave could match the bed and cushion of the gale?

This storm tossed the wave and the stones of the sea-wall up together. The next day it left the waters white with the thrilling whiteness of foam in sunshine. It was only the Channel; and in such narrow waters you do not see the distances, the wide levels of fleeting and floating foam, that lie light between long wave and long wave on a Mediterranean coast, regions of delicate and transitory brightness so far out that all the waves, near and far, seem to be breaking at the same moment, one beyond the other, and league beyond league, into foam. But the Channel has its own strong, short curl that catches the rushing shingle up with the freshest of all noises and runs up with sudden curves, white upon the white sea-wall, under the random shadow of sea-gulls and the light of a shining cloud.

THE DAFFODIL

To travel eastwards and breast the sun, to sail towards the watershed and breast the floods, to go north and breast the winter--fresh and warm are the energies of such bracing action; but more animating still is it to live so as to breast the stress of time.

Man and woman may, like the child, or almost like him, fill the time and enlarge the capacity of the day--our poor day that so easily shrinks and dwindles in the careless possession of idle minds. The date, every first of March, for example, may sweep upon a large curve and come home annually after a swinging flight. To the infinite variety of natural days may be entrusted half the work of strengthening the flight against time, but the other half must be the task of the vehement heart. Nature assuredly does not fail. Days, seasons, and years are as wide asunder as the unforeseen can set them, and a crowd of children is not more various. But the resisting heart seems of late to be somewhat lacking. We are inclined to turn our heel upon the East, upon the watershed, upon the gates of the wind, and to go the smooth road.

We are even precipitate, and whip our way faster on the time-killing course than the natural event would take us. It is not enough that we should run helplessly, we outstrip the breeze and outsail the current with the ease of our untimely luxuries. Our daffodils are no longer to have the praise of their daring, for we no longer relate them to the lagging swallow. By the time the barely budding woods give a poor man's lodging to the cold daffodil--a scanty kind taking the wind with a short stalk and giving it but small petals to buffet--we have already said farewell to the tall and splendid green-house daffodil that never braved the cold. We gave to this our untimely welcome long before the snowdrop came, and the golden name of daffodil has lost its vernal sound. And when we part with the improved creature, lofty and enlarged, we hardly know or care whether the starveling is yet mustering in hollows of woodlands, or whether it is over or to come. We are attending to a yellower tulip, no doubt, when the only daffodil that Shakespeare knew is opening in the chilly wood.

The reproach is a commonplace, but perhaps we have generally accused ourselves of the impatience rather than of the listlessness, and have not noted how we shorten the disarranged seasons and lay up for ourselves memories confused and undefined. Late springs and early, gentle and hard, are compelled to yield the same colours; haste has its way and its revenges. If we are resolved to live quickly, why, nothing is easier. There are no such brief days as those that are indistinct; and the sliding on the way of time is, of all habits, the most tyrannously careless. It is first a laxity, then a habit, and next a folly; and when we keep neither Ash Wednesday nor the birthday of daffodils, and have hardly felt the cold, and do not know where the sun rises, we are already on the way of least resistance, the friction of life is gone; and in our last old age the past will seem to dwindle even like the dwindled present of our decline.

There has been one unconscious operation of the love of life, one single grasp after variety, intended to save the year, to face it, to meet it, to compel it to show a unique face and bear a name of its own; and this is travel. It is the finest and most effectual flight against time of all. What elastic days are those wherein I make head against a travelling landscape, meet histories and boundaries, hail frontiers, face a new manner of building, cross the regions of silver roofs and of heavy Alpine stone, and bring with me the late light upon billowy gables and red eaves! And how buoyant the week in which I anticipate the sun upon the roofless east! How serried are the days with forests, how enlarged by plains, how thronged by cities, how singled by the pine, how newly audible by a new sea! Far was the sunrise from the sunset, and noon is one memorable midday with shortened shadows upon some solitary road.

Our fathers had friction of another kind: hardship at home, winters and nights that were dark with a darkness we have abolished; springs that brought an infinite releasing, illumination, and recolouring. None of us has seen the sight, or breathed the air, or heard those emancipated voices. The bloom, the birds, the ifted sky! Bright nights and glowing houses have surely robbed us of that variety, and all these untimely fruits and flowers have suppressed even the small privations of a winter in disguise.

In those days Englishmen had to breast the times as they were. They had the privilege of their latitude--vigorous and rigorous seasons. They had a year full of change--their time was stretched whether with impatience or with patience, with conflict or with felicity. Their salt meats were not the worst of it; there was the siege of darkness, the captivity of cold, the threat of storm, and the labour to close with the closing enemy, to break ways and save animals alive, and keep the laws in force in the street in the long and secret nights. From such a season of winter at home, winter well known, men broke free to hail their daffodils. They found them, short, strong, and shivering, in the still open and undefended woods. In the springs before Chaucer, and earlier than the day of the first spring lyric, in the same places grew the keen wild flowers as now; but they assuredly were marked with another welcome; they made memories; this year's wild harvest was not confused with that of last year, or of half-a-score of years gone by. Distance of vital time set the springs far apart, and made the daffodils strangers.

They were greeted with the courtesy due to strangers, so fresh must have been the senses of the villager, and of the citizen of the village town. Suburbs divide a city from the fields as walls did never. He of old went from a little town, close and serried as a new box of toys, with one step into the unsmirched country, carrying an unsated heart. Refreshed with the animating compulsion of changeful life were man and woman, and much like their child in a constant capacity for unique experiences, unique days, years that are separate, known, and distinguishable, and not only separate but long.

Indeed, some of us who travel hardly know how to remedy our fugitive, resembling, hastening, and collapsing seasons, even by means of this sovereign remedy of travel. It is to be feared that a modern journey is not always to us so bracing a manner of living as was the untravelled journey of hard days at home to the ancient islander. To journey as he did, keeping his feet, with a moving heart against the moving seasons, to resist, to withstand, widened the hours; but his posterity are taking all means to narrow their own, even on the railway. To go the same way every year, for instance, is to lose, when a few such years are gone, nearly all the gain to life. To take no heed at all of the way, but merely to be by any means at the end of the travelling, to sleep or go by night, and to calculate Europe by hours, half-hours, junctions, and dining-cars, is but to close up the time as though you closed a telescope. A long railway journey and a long motor journey may be taken with the flight of time as well as against it, and the habit of summaries can use these too to its own end. Precipitate, unresisting, are the day in the train and the heedless night. We love to reproach ourselves with living at too great a speed, having, perhaps, no sense of the second meaning of the phrase. Medicine may, perhaps, fulfil her promise of giving us a few more years, but habit derides her by making each year a scanty gift.

Much, too, of the spirit of time is lost to us because we will not let the sun rule the day. He would see to it that our hours were various; but we have preferred to his various face the plain face of a clock, and the lights without vicissitudes of our nights without seasons.

ADDRESSES

Not free from some ignominious attendance upon the opinion of the world is he who too consciously withdraws his affairs from its judgements. He is indebted to "the public." He is at least indebted to it for the fact that there is, yonder, without, a public. Lacking this excluded multitude his fastidiousness would have no subject, and his singularity no contrast. He would, in his grosser moods, have nothing to refuse, and nothing, in his finer, to ignore.

He, at any rate, is one, and the rest are numerous. They minister to him popular errors. But if they are nothing else in regard to himself, they are many. If he must have distinction, it is there on easy terms--he is one.

Well for him if he does not contract the heavier debt shouldered by the man who owes to the unknown, un-named, and uncounted his pleasure in their conjectured or implicit envy; who conceives the jealousy they may have covertly to endure, enjoys it, and thus silently begins and ends within his own morosity the story of his base advantage.

Vanity has indignity as its underside. And how shall even the pleasure in beauty be altogether without it? For since beauty, like other human things, is comparative, how shall the praise, or the admiration, thereof be free from (at least) some reference to the unbeautiful? Or from some allusion to the less beautiful? Yet this, if inevitable, is little; it may be negligible. The triumph of beauty is all but innocent. It is where no beauty is in question that lurks the unconfessed appeal to envy. That appeal is not an appeal to admiration--it lacks what is the genial part of egoism. For who, except perhaps a recent writer of articles on society in America, really admires a man for living in the approved part of Boston?

The vanity of addresses is as frequent with us as on the western side of the Atlantic. It is a vanity without that single apology for vanity--gaiety of heart. The first things that are, in London, sacrificed to it are the beautiful day and the facing of the sky. There are some amongst us whose wives have constrained them to dwell underground for love of an address. Modern and foolish is that contempt for daylight. To the simple, day is beautiful; and "beautiful as day" a happy proverb.

Over all colour, flesh, aspect, surface, manifestation of vitality, dwells one certain dominance. And if One, vigilant for the dues of His vicegerent, should ask us whose is the image and superscription? We reply, The Sun's.

The London air shortens and clips those beams, and yet leaves daylight the finest thing we know. Beauty of artificial lights is in our streets at night, but their chief beauty is when, just before night, they adorn the day. The late daylight honours them when it so easily and sweetly subdues and overcomes them, giving to the electric lamp, to the taper, to the hearth fire, and to the spark, a loveliness not their own.

With the unpublished desire to be envied, whereto here and there amongst us is sacrificed the sky, abides the desire for an object of unconfessed contempt. Both are contrary to that more authentic, that essential solitariness wherein a few men have the grace to live, and wherein all men are compelled to die. Both are unpublished even now, even in our days, when it costs men so little to manifest the effrontery of their opinions.

The difference between our worldliness and the New-worldliness is chiefly that here we are apt to remove, by a little space, the distinction brought about by riches, to put it back, to interpose, between it and our actual life, a generation or two, an education or two. Obviously, it was riches that made the class differences, if not now, then a little time ago. Therefore the New England citizen should not be reproved by us for anything except his too great candour. A social guide-book to some city of the Republic is in my hands. I note how the very names of streets take a sound of veneration or of cheerful derision from the writer's pen. It is evident that the names are almost enough. They have an expression. He is like a *naif* teller of humorous anecdotes, who cannot keep his own smiles in order till he have done.

This social writer has scorn, as an author should, and he wreaks it upon parishes. He turns me a phrase with the northern end of a town and makes an epigram of the southern. He caps a sarcasm with an address.

In truth, we too might write social guide-books to the same effect, had we the same simplicity. It is to be thought that we too hold an address, be it a good one, so closely that if Fortune should see fit to snatch it from us, she must needs do so with violence. Such unseemly violence, in this as in other transactions, is ours in the clinging and not hers in the taking. For equal is the force of Fortune, and steady is her grasp, whether she despoil the great of their noble things or strip the mean of things ignoble, whether she take from the clutching or the yielding hand.

Strange are the little traps laid by the Londoner so as to capture an address by the hem if he may. You would think a good address to be of all blessings the most stationary, and one to be either gained or missed, and no two ways about it. But not so. You shall see it waylaid at the angles of squares, with no slight exercise of skill, delayed, entreated, detained, entangled, intricately caught, persuaded to round a corner, prolonged beyond all probability, pursued.

One address there will in the future be for us, and few will visit there. It will bear the number of a narrow house. May it avow its poverty and be poor; for the obscure inhabitant, in frigid humility, shall have no thought nor no eye askance upon the multitude.

THE AUDIENCE

The long laugh that sometimes keeps the business of the stage waiting is only a sign of the exchange of parts that in the theatre every night takes place. The audience are the players. Their audience on the stage are bound to watch them, to understand them, to anticipate them, and to divine them. But once known and their character established in relation to a particular play, the audience--what is called the audience--need give no further trouble. They themselves cannot alter; they are fixed and compelled by the tremendous force of averages. The most inexorable of laws, and the most irresistible of necessities are upon them; they cannot do otherwise; they are out of the reach of accidents; they are made fast in their own mediocrity. They are a thousand London people; and no genius, or no imbecility, amongst them has any effect upon that secure sovereignty of a number.

The long laugh generally means that the house--by its unalterable majority--has laughed at one joke three times. The stage waits upon the audience, and the audience rehearses its collective and inevitable laugh. It performs. It communicates itself, and art is a communication. A small and chosen party is made up, behind the footlights, to see a thousand people, given helpless into the hands of destiny and subject to averages, so express themselves.

The audience's audience (the people on the stage) are persuaded into applauding the laugh too long and too often. The author is, of course, one of them, and he applauds by making too many such translations. They are perhaps worth making, and even worth renewing in acknowledgement of a smile; but it is surely to encourage the house unduly to make them so important. The actors applaud their audience by repeating--and not once or only twice--a piece of comic business. Does the Average laugh so well as indeed to deserve all this?

The Average does little more than laugh. It knows that its own truest talents are indubitably comic. We have no real tragic audiences. This is no expression of regret over legitimate audiences, or audiences of the old school, or any audiences of that kind, whose day may or may not have had a date. It is a mere statement of the fact that audiences have lost, or never had, a distinguishing perception of emotion, whereas they have every kind of perception of humour, distinguishing and general. Their laugh never fails. If their friends behind would really care to improve them, it might be done by exacting from them a little more temperance in their sense of comedy. We shall never have a really good school of audience without the exercise of some such severity.

For obviously when we call an average unchangeable, we mean that it is unchangeable for its time merely. There might be a slow upraising of the level. It would still be a level, and there would still be a compelling law upon one thousand that it should do the same thing as another thousand; but that same thing might become somewhat more intelligent.

When a fine actor does a fine thing, have we such a school of audience as to merit this admirable supply to their demands?--this applause of their understanding? Is there not in the whole excellent piece of work, something all too independent of their part in the theatre?

If Caligula wished that mankind had but one neck for his knife, and Byron that all womankind had but one mouth for his kiss, so the audience has conceived that all arts should have but one mystery for its blundering, and thus thinks itself interested in acting when it does but admire the actor as in a drawing.

The time may come when a national school of dramatic audience shall not accept artifices that could not convince the fool amongst them; when one brilliant moment of simplicity on the one side of the footlights shall meet a brilliant simplicity on the other. Which troupe, which side, to begin?

TITHONUS

"It was resolved," said the morning paper, "to colour the borders of the panels and other spaces of Portland stone with arabesques and other patterns, but that no paint should be used, as paint would need renewing from time to time. The colours, therefore,"--and here is the passage to be noted--"are all mixed with wax liquefied with petroleum; and the wax surface sets as hard as marble. . . The wax is left time to form an imperishable surface of ornament, which would have to be cut out of the stone with a chisel if it was desired to remove it." Not, apparently, that a new surface is formed which, by much violence and perseverance, could, years hence, be chipped off again; but that the "ornament" is driven in and incorporate, burnt in and absorbed, so that there is nothing possible to cut away by any industry. In this humorous form of ornament we are beforehand with Posterity. Posterity is baffled.

Will this victory over our sons' sons be the last resolute tyranny prepared by one age for the coercion, constraint, and defeat of the future? To impose that compulsion has been hitherto one of the strongest of human desires. It is one, doubtless, to be outgrown by the human race; but how slowly that growth creeps onwards, let this success in the stencilling of St Paul's teach us, to our confusion. There is evidently a man--a group of men--happy at this moment because it has been possible, by great ingenuity, to force our posterity to have their cupola of St Paul's with the stone mouldings stencilled and "picked out" with niggling colours, whether that undefended posterity like it or not. And this is a survival of one of the obscure pleasures of man, attested by history.

It is impossible to read the Thirty-nine Articles, for example, and not to recognize in those acts of final, all-resolute, eager, eternal legislation one of the strongest of all recorded proofs of this former human wish. If Galileo's Inquisitors put a check upon the earth, which yet moved, a far bolder enterprise was the Reformers' who arrested the moving man, and inhibited the moving God. The sixteenth century and a certain part of the age immediately following seem to be times when the desire had conspicuously become a passion. Say the middle of the sixteenth century in Italy and the beginning of the seventeenth in England--for in those days we were somewhat in the rear. ***There*** is the obstinate, confident, unreluctant, undoubting, and resolved seizure upon power. ***Then*** was Rome rebuilt, re-faced, marked with a single sign and style. Then was many a human hand stretched forth to grasp the fate of the unborn. The fortunes and the thoughts of the day to come were to be as the day then present would have them, if the dead hand--the living hand that was then to die, and was to keep its hold in death--could by any means make them fast.

Obviously, to build at all is to impose something upon an age that may be more than willing to build for itself. The day may soon come when no man will do even so much without some impulse of apology. Posterity is not compelled to keep our pictures or our books in existence, nor to read nor to look at them; but it is more or less obliged to have a stone building in view for an age or two. We can hardly avoid some of the forms of tyranny over the future, but few, few are the living men who would consent to share in this horrible ingenuity at St Paul's--this petroleum and this wax.

In 1842 they were discussing the decoration of the Houses of Parliament, and the efforts of all in council were directed upon the future. How the frescoes then to be achieved by the artists of the day should be made secure against all mischances--smoke, damp, "the risk of bulging," even accidents attending the washing of upper floors--all was discussed in confidence with the public. It was impossible for anyone who read the papers then to escape from some at least of the responsibilities of technical knowledge. From Genoa, from Rome, from Munich especially, all kinds of expert and most deliberate schemes were gathered in order to defeat the natural and not superfluous operation of efficient and effacing time.

The academic little capital of Bavaria had, at about the same date, decorated a vast quantity of wall space of more than one order of architecture. Art revived and was encouraged at that time and place with unparalleled obstinacy. They had not the malice of the petroleum that does violence to St Paul's; but they had instead an indomitable patience. Under the commands of the master Cornelius, they baffled time and all his work--refused his pardons, his absolutions, his cancelling indulgences--by a perseverance that nothing could discourage. Who has not known somewhat indifferent painters mighty busy about their colours and varnishes? Cornelius caused a pit to be dug for the preparation of the lime, and in the case of the Ludwig Kirche this lime remained there for eight years, with frequent stirrings. This was in order that the whole fresco, when at last it was entrusted to its bed, should be set there for immortality. Nor did the master fail to thwart time by those mechanical means that should avert the risk of bulging already mentioned. He neglected no detail. He was provident, and he lay in wait for more than one of the laws of nature, to frustrate them. Gravitation found him prepared, and so did the less majestic but not vain dispensation of accidents. Against bulging he had an underplot of tiles set on end; against possible trickling from an upper floor he had asphalt; it was all part of the human conspiracy. In effect, the dull pictures at Munich seem to stand well. It would have been more just--so the present age thinks of these preserved walls--if the day that admired them had had them exclusively, and our day had been exempt. The painted cathedrals of the Middle Ages have undergone the natural correction; why not the Ludwig Kirche?

In 1842, then, the nations were standing, as it were, shoulder to shoulder against the walk of time and against his gentle act and art. They had just called iron into their cabal. Cornelius came from Munich to London, looked at the walls at Westminster, and put a heart of confidence into the breast of the Commission. The situation, he averred, need not be too damp for immortality, with due care. What he had done in the Glyptothek and in the Pinacothek might be done with the best results in England, in defiance of the weather, of the river, of the mere days, of the divine order of alteration, and, in a word, of heaven and earth.

Meanwhile, there was that good servant of the law of change, lime that had not been kept quite long enough, ready to fulfil its mission; they would have none of it. They evaded it, studied its ways, and put it to the rout. "Many failures that might have been hastily attributed to damp were really owing to the use of lime in too fresh a state. Of the experimental works painted at Munich, those only have faded which are known to have been done without due attention to the materials. Thus, a figure of Bavaria, painted by Kaulbach, which has faded considerably, is known to have been executed with lime that was too fresh." One cannot refrain from italics: the way was so easy; it was only to take a little less of this important care about the lime, to have a better confidence, to be more impatient and eager, and all had been well: *not* to do--a virtue of omission.

This is not a matter of art-criticism. It is an ethical question hitherto unstudied. The makers of laws have not always been obliged to face it, inasmuch as their laws are made in part for the present, and in part for that future whereof the present needs to be assured--that is, the future is bound as a guaranty for present security of person or property. Some such hold upon the time to come we are obliged to claim, and to claim it for our own sakes--because of the reflex effect upon our own affairs, and not for the pleasure of fettering the time to come. Every maker of a will does at least this.

Were the men of the sixteenth century so moderate? Not they. They found the present all too narrow for the imposition of their will. It did not satisfy them to disinter and scatter the bones of the dead, nor to efface the records of a past that offended them. It did not satisfy them to bind the present to obedience by imperative menace and instant compulsion. When they had burnt libraries and thrown down monuments and pursued the rebels of the past into the other world, and had seen to it that none living should evade them, then they outraged the future.

Whatever misgivings may have visited those dominant minds as to the effectual and final success of their measures--would their writ run in time as well as place, and were the nameless populations indeed their subjects?--whatever questions may have peered in upon those rigid counsels and upon those busy vigils of the keepers of the world, they silenced by legislation and yet more legislation. They wrote in statute books; they would have written their will across the skies. Their hearts would have burnt for lack of records more inveterate, and of testimonials that mankind should lack courage to question, if in truth they did ever doubt lest posterity might try their lock. Perhaps they did never so much as foresee the race of the unnumbered and emancipated for whom their prohibitions and penalties are no more than documents of history.

If the tyrannous day of our fathers had but possessed the means of these our more diffident times! They, who would have written their present and actual will upon the skies, might certainly have written it in petroleum and wax upon the stone. Fate did them wrong in withholding from their hands this means of finality and violence. Into our hands it has been given at a time when the student of the race thought, perhaps, that we had been proved in the school of forbearance. Something, indeed, we may have learnt therein, but not enough, as we now find.

We have not yet the natural respect for the certain knowledge and the probable wisdom of our successors. A certain reverend official document, not guiltless of some confusion of thought, lately recommended to the veneration of the present times "those past ages with their store of experience." Doubtless, as the posterity of their predecessors our predecessors had experience, but, as our ancestors, none--none. Therefore, if they were a little reverend our own posterity is right reverend. It is a flippant and novelty-loving humour that so flatters the unproved past and refuses the deference due to the burden of years which is ours, which--grown still graver--will be our children's.

THE TOW PATH

A childish pleasure in producing small mechanical effects unaided must have some part in the sense of enterprise wherewith you gird your shoulders with the tackle, and set out, alone but necessary, on the even path of the lopped and grassy side of the Thames--the side of meadows.

The elastic resistance of the line is a "heart-animating strain," only too slight; and sensible is the thrill in it as the ranks of the riverside plants, with their small summit-flower of violet-pink, are swept aside like a long green breaker of flourishing green. The line drums lightly in the ears when the bushes are high and it grows taut; it makes a telephone for the rush of flowers under the stress of your easy power.

The active delights of one who is not athletic are few, like the joys of "feeling hearts" according to the erroneous sentiment of a verse of Moore's. The joys of sensitive hearts are many; but the joys of sensitive hands are few. Here, however, in the effectual act of towing, is the ample revenge of the unmuscular upon the happy labourers with the oar, the pole, the bicycle, and all other means of violence. Here, on the long tow-path, between warm, embrowned meadows and opal waters, you need but to walk in your swinging harness, and so take your friends upstream.

You work merely as the mill-stream works--by simple movement. At lock after lock along a hundred miles, deep-roofed mills shake to the wheel that turns by no greater stress, and you and the river have the same mere force of progress.

There never was any kinder incentive of companionship. It is the bright Thames walking softly in your blood, or you that are flowing by so many curves of low shore on the level of the world.

Now you are over against the shadows, and now opposite the sun, as the wheeling river makes the sky wheel about your head and swings the lighted clouds or the blue to face your eyes. The birds, flying high for mountain air in the heat, wing nothing but their own weight. You will not envy them for so brief a success. Did not Wordsworth want a "little boat" for the air? Did not Byron call him a blockhead therefor? Wordsworth had, perhaps, a sense of towing.

All the advantage of the expert is nothing in this simple industry. Even the athlete, though he may go further, cannot do better than you, walking your effectual walk with the line attached to your willing steps. Your moderate strength of a mere everyday physical education gives you the sufficient mastery of the towpath.

If your natural walk is heavy, there is spirit in the tackle to give it life, and if it is buoyant it will be more buoyant under the buoyant burden--the yielding check--than ever before. An unharnessed walk must begin to seem to you a sorry incident of insignificant liberty. It is easier than towing? So is the drawing of water in a sieve easier to the arms than drawing in a bucket, but not to the heart.

To walk unbound is to walk in prose, without the friction of the wings of metre, without the sweet and encouraging tug upon the spirit and the line.

No dead weight follows you as you tow. The burden is willing; it depends upon you gaily, as a friend may do without making any depressing show of helplessness; neither, on the other hand, is it apt to set you at naught or charge you with a make-believe. It accompanies, it almost anticipates; it lags when you are brisk, just so much as to give your briskness good reason, and to justify you if you should take to still more nimble heels. All your haste, moreover, does but waken a more brilliantly-sounding ripple.

The bounding and rebounding burden you carry (but it nearly seems to carry you, so fine is the mutual good will) gives work to your figure, enlists your erectness and your gait, but leaves your eyes free. No watching of mechanisms for the labourer of the tow-path. What little outlook is to be kept falls to the lot of the steerer smoothly towed. Your easy and efficient work lets you carry your head high and watch the birds, or listen to them. They fly in such lofty air that they seem to turn blue in the blue sky. A flash of their flight shows silver for a moment, but they are blue birds in that sunny distance above, as mountains are blue, and horizons. The days are so still that you do not merely hear the cawing of the rooks--you overhear their hundred private croakings and creakings, the soliloquy of the solitary places swept by wings.

As for songs, it is September, and the silence of July is long at an end. This year's robins are in full voice; and the only song that is not for love or nesting--the childish song of boy-birds, the freshest and youngest note--is, by a happy paradox, that of an autumnal voice.

Here is no hoot, nor hurry of engines, nor whisper of the cyclist's wheel, nor foot upon a road, to overcome that light but resounding note. Silent are feet on the grassy brink, like the innocent, stealthy soles of the barefooted in the south.

THE TETHERED CONSTELLATIONS

It is no small thing--no light discovery--to find a river Andromeda and Arcturus and their bright neighbours wheeling for half a summer night around a pole-star in the waters. One star or two--delicate visitants of streams--we are used to see, somewhat by a sleight of the eyes, so fine and so fleeting is that apparition. Or the southern waves may show the light--not the image--of the evening or the morning planet. But this, in a pool of the country Thames at night, is no ripple-lengthened light; it is the startling image of a whole large constellation burning in the flood.

These reflected heavens are different heavens. On a darker and more vacant field than that of the real skies, the shape of the Lyre or the Bear has an altogether new and noble solitude; and the waters play a painter's part in setting their splendid subject free. Two movements shake but do not scatter the still night: the bright flashing of constellations in the deep Weir-pool, and the dark flashes of the vague bats flying. The stars in the stream fluctuate with an alien motion. Reversed, estranged, isolated, every shape of large stars escapes and returns, escapes and returns. Fitful in the steady night, those constellations, so few, so whole, and so remote, have a suddenness of gleaming life. You imagine that some unexampled gale might make them seem to shine with such a movement in the veritable sky; yet nothing but deep water, seeming still in its incessant flight and rebound, could really show such altered stars. The flood lets a constellation fly, as Juliet's "wanton" with a tethered bird, only to pluck it home again. At moments some rhythmic flux of the water seems about to leave the darkly-set, widely-spaced Bear absolutely at large, to dismiss the great stars, and refuse to imitate the skies, and all the water is obscure; then one broken star returns, then fragments of another, and a third and a fourth flit back to their noble places, brilliantly vague, wonderfully visible, mobile, and unalterable. There is nothing else at once so keen and so elusive.

The aspen poplar had been in captive flight all day, but with no such vanishings as these. The dimmer constellations of the soft night are reserved by the skies. Hardly is a secondary star seen by the large and vague eyes of the stream. They are blind to the Pleiades.

There is a little kind of star that drowns itself by hundreds in the river Thames--the many-rayed silver-white seed that makes journeys on all the winds up and down England and across it in the end of summer. It is a most expert traveller, turning a little wheel a-tiptoe wherever the wind lets it rest, and speeding on those pretty points when it is not

flying. The streets of London are among its many highways, for it is
fragile enough to go far in all sorts of weather. But it gets disabled
if a rough gust tumbles it on the water so that its finely-feathered feet
are wet. On gentle breezes it is able to cross dry-shod, walking the
waters.

All unlike is this pilgrim star to the tethered constellations. It is
far adrift. It goes singly to all the winds. It offers thistle plants
(or whatever is the flower that makes such delicate ashes) to the tops of
many thousand hills. Doubtless the farmer would rather have to meet it
in battalions than in these invincible units astray. But if the farmer
owes it a lawful grudge, there is many a rigid riverside garden wherein
it would be a great pleasure to sow the thistles of the nearest pasture.

POPULAR BURLESQUE

The more I consider that strange inversion of idolatry which is the
motive of Guy Fawkes Day and which annually animates the by-streets with
the sound of processionals and of recessionals--a certain popular version
of "Lest we forget" their unvaried theme; the more I hear the cries of
derision raised by the makers of this likeness of something unworshipful
on the earth beneath, so much the more am I convinced that the national
humour is that of banter, and that no other kind of mirth so gains as
does this upon the public taste.

Here, for example, is the popular idea of a street festival; that day is
as the people will actually have it, with their own invention, their own
material, their own means, and their own spirit. They owe nothing on
this occasion to the promptings or the subscriptions of the classes that

are apt to take upon themselves the direction and tutelage of the people in relation to any form of art. Here on every fifth of November the people have their own way with their own art; and their way is to offer the service of the image-maker, reversed in hissing and irony, to some creature of their hands.

It is a wanton fancy; and perhaps no really barbarous people is capable of so overturning the innocent plan of original portraiture. To make a mental image of all things that are named to the ear, or conceived in the mind, being an industrious custom of children and childish people which lapses in the age of much idle reading, the making of a material image is the still more diligent and more sedulous act, whereby the primitive man controls and caresses his own fancy. He may take arms anon, disappointed, against his own work; but did he ever do that work in malice from the outset?

From the statue to the doll, images are all outraged in the person of the guy. If it were but an antithesis to the citizen's idea of something admirable which he might carry in procession on some other day, the carrying of the guy would be less gloomy; but he would hoot at a suspicion that he might admire anything so much as to make a good-looking doll in its praise. There is absolutely no image-making art in the practice of our people, except only this art of rags and contumely. Or, again, if the revenge taken upon a guy were that of anger for a certain cause, the destruction would not be the work of so thin an annual malice and of so heartless a rancour.

But the single motive is that popular irony which becomes daily--or so it seems--more and more the holiday temper of the majority. Mockery is the only animating impulse, and a loud incredulity is the only intelligence. They make an image of some one in whom they do not believe, to deride it. Say that the guy is the effigy of an agitator in the cause of something to be desired; the street man and boy have then two motives of mocking:

they think the reform to be not worth doing, and they are willing to suspect the reformer of some kind of hypocrisy. Perhaps the guy of this occasion is most characteristic of all guys in London. The people, having him or her to deride, do not even wait for the opportunity of their annual procession. They anticipate time, and make an image when it is not November, and sell it at the market of the kerb.

Hear, moreover, the songs which some nameless one makes for the citizens, perhaps in thoughtful renunciation of the making of their laws. These, too, seem to have for their inspiration the universal taunt. They are, indeed, most in vogue when they have no meaning at all--this it is that makes the *succes fou* (and here Paris is of one mind with London) of the street; but short of such a triumph, and when a meaning is discernible, it is an irony.

Bank Holiday courtship (if the inappropriate word can be pardoned) seems to be done, in real life, entirely by banter. And it is the strangest thing to find that the banter of women by men is the most mocking in the exchange. If the burlesque of the maid's tongue is provocative, that of the man's is derisive. Somewhat of the order of things as they stood before they were inverted seems to remain, nevertheless, as a memory; nay, to give the inversion a kind of lagging interest. Irony is made more complete by the remembrance, and by an implicit allusion to the state of courtship in other classes, countries, or times. Such an allusion no doubt gives all its peculiar twang to the burlesque of love.

With the most strange submission these Englishwomen in their millions undergo all degrees of derision from the tongues of men who are their mates, equals, contemporaries, perhaps in some obscure sense their suitors, and in a strolling manner, with one knows not what ungainly motive of reserve, even their admirers. Nor from their tongues only; for, to pass the time, the holiday swain annoys the girl; and if he wears her hat, it is ten to one that he has plucked it off with a humorous disregard of her dreadful pins.

We have to believe that unmocked love has existence in the streets, because of the proof that is published when a man shoots a woman who has rejected him; and from this also do we learn to believe that a woman of the burlesque classes is able to reject. But for that sign we should find little or nothing intelligible in what we see or overhear of the drama of love in popular life.

In its easy moments, in its leisure, at holiday time, it baffles all tradition, and shows us the spirit of comedy clowning after a fashion that is insular and not merely civic. You hear the same twang in country places; and whether the English maid, having, like the antique, thrown her apple at her shepherd, run into the thickets of Hampstead Heath or among sylvan trees, it seems that the most humorous thing to be done by the swain would be, in the opinion in vogue, to stroll another way. Insular I have said, because I have not seen the like of this fashion whether in America or elsewhere in Europe.

But the chief inversion of all, proved summarily by the annual inversion of the worship of images on the fifth of November, is that of a sentence of Wordsworth's--"We live by admiration."

DRY AUTUMN

One who has much and often protested against the season of Autumn, her pathos, her chilly breakfast-time, her "tints," her decay, and her extraordinary popularity, saw cause one year to make a partial recantation. Autumn, until then, had seemed to be a practitioner of all the easy arts at once, or rather, she had taken the easy way with the arts of colour, sentiment, suggestion, and regret.

She had often encouraged and rewarded, also, the ingratitude of a whole nation for a splendid summer, somewhat officiously cooling, refreshing, allaying, and comforting the discontent of the victims of an English sun. She had soothed the fuming citizen, and brought back the fogs of custom, effaced the skies, to which he had upturned no very attentive eye, muffled up his chin, and in many other ways curried favour. Not only did she fall in with his landscape mood, but she made herself his housemate by his fireplaces, drew his curtains, shut out her own wet winds in the streets, and became privy to the commoner comforts of man, like a wild creature tamed and conniving at human sport and schemes. "Domesticated" Gothic itself, or the governesses who daily by advertisement describe themselves by that same strange modern adjective, could not be more bent upon the flattery of man in his less heroic moments.

Autumn, for all her show of stormy woods, is apt to be the accomplice of daily human things that lack dignity, and are, in the now accepted sense of a once noble word, comfortable. Besides, her show of stormy forests is done with an abandonment to the pathos of the moment, with dashings and underlinings--we all know the sort of letter, for instance, which answers to the message and proclamation of Autumn, as she usually is in the outer world. A complete sentimentalist is she, whether in the open country or when she looks in at the lighted windows, and goodnaturedly makes her voice like a very goblin's outside, for the increasing of the bourgeois' **bien-etre**.

But that year all had been otherwise. Autumn had borne herself with a heroism of sunny weather. Where we had been wont to see signals of distress, and to hear the voluble outpouring of an excitable temperament, with the extremity of scattered leaves and desperate damp, we beheld an aspect of golden drought. Nothing mouldered--everything was consumed by vital fires. The gardens were strewn with smouldering soft ashes of late roses, late honeysuckle, honey-sweet clematis. The silver seeds of rows of riverside flowers took sail on their random journey with a light wind. Leaves set forth, a few at a time, with a little volley of birds--a buoyant caravel. Or, in the stiller weather, the infrequent fall of leaves took place quietly, with no proclamation of ruin, in the privacy within the branches. While nearly all the woods were still fresh as streams, you might see that here or there was one, with an invincible summer smile, slowly consuming, in defiance of decay. Life destroyed that autumn, not death.

The novelist would be at a loss had we a number of such years. He would lose the easiest landscape--for the autumn has among her facile ways the way of allowing herself to be described by rote. But there were no regions of crimson woods and yellow--only the grave, cool, and cheerful green of the health of summer, and now and then that deep bronzing of the leaves that the sun brought to pass. Never did apples look better than in those still vigorous orchards. They shone so that lamps would hardly be brighter. The apple-gathering, under such a sun, was nearly as warm and brilliant as a vintage; and indeed it was of the Italian autumn that you were reminded. There were the same sunburnt tones, the same brown health. There was the dark smile of chestnut woods as among the Apennines.

For it was chiefly within the woods that the splendid autumn without pathos gave delight. The autumn *with* pathos has a way there of overwhelming her many fragrances in the general odour of dead leaves generalized. That year you could breathe all the several sweet scents, as discriminated and distinct as those of flowers on the tops of mountains--warm pine and beech as different as thyme and broom, unconfused. Even the Spring, with her little divided breezes of hawthorn, rose, and lilac, was not more various.

Moreover, while some of the woods were green, none of the fields were so. In their sunburnt colours were to be seen "autumn tints" of a far different beauty from that of a gaudy decay. Dry autumn is a general lover of simplicity, and she sweeps a landscape with long plain colours that take their variations from the light. When the country looks "burnt up," as they say who are ungrateful for the sun, then are these colours most tender. Grass, that had lost its delicacy in the day when the last hay was carried, gets it again. For a little time it was--new-reaped--of something too hard a green; then came dry autumn along, and softened it into a hundred exquisite browns. Dry autumn does beautiful things in sepia, as the water-colour artist did in the early days, and draws divine brown Turners of the first manner.

The fields and hedgerows must needs fade, and the sun made the fading quick with the bloom of brown. For one great meadow so softly gilded, I would give all the scarlet and yellow trees that ever made a steaming autumn gorgeous--all the crimson of the Rhine valleys, all the patched and spotted walnut-leaves of the ***muhl-thal*** by Boppard, and the little trees that change so suddenly to their yellow of decay in groups at the foot of the ruins of Sternberg and Liebenstein, every one of their branches disguised in the same bright, insignificant, unhopeful colour.

An autumn so rare should not close without a recorded "hail and farewell!" Spring was not braver, summer was not sweeter. That year's great sun called upon a great spirit in all the riverside woods. Those woods did not grow cold; they yielded to their last sunset.

THE PLAID

It is disconcerting to hear of the plaid in India. Our dyes, we know, they use in the silk mills of Bombay, with the deplorable result that their old clothes are dull and unintentionally falsified with infelicitous decay. The Hindus are a washing people; and the sun and water that do but dim, soften, and warm the native vegetable dyes to the last, do but burlesque the aniline. Magenta is bad enough when it is itself; but the worst of magenta is that it spoils but poorly. No bad modern forms and no bad modern colours spoil well. And spoiling is an important process. It is a test--one of the ironical tests that come too late with their proofs. London portico-houses will make some such ruins as do chemical dyes, which undergo no use but derides them, no accidents but caricature them. This is an old enough grievance. But the plaid!

The plaid is the Scotchman's contribution to the decorative art of the world. Scotland has no other indigenous decoration. In his most admirable lecture on "The Two Paths," Ruskin acknowledged, with a passing misgiving, that his Highlanders had little art. And the misgiving was but passing, because he considered how fatally wrong was the art of India--"it never represents a natural fact. It forms its compositions out of meaningless fragments of colour and flowings of line . . . It will not draw a man, but an eight-armed monster; it will not draw a flower, but only a spiral or a zig-zag." Because of this aversion from Nature the Hindu and his art tended to evil, we read. But of the Scot we are told, "You will find upon reflection that all the highest points of the Scottish character are connected with impressions derived straight from the natural scenery of their country."

What, then, about the plaid? Where is the natural fact there? If the

Ceres' Runaway

Indian, by practising a non-natural art of spirals and zig-zags, cuts himself off "from all possible sources of healthy knowledge or natural delight," to what did the good and healthy Highlander condemn himself by practising the art of the plaid? A spiral may be found in the vine, and a zig-zag in the lightning, but where in nature is the plaid to be found? There is surely no curve or curl that can be drawn by a designing hand but is a play upon some infinitely various natural fact. The smoke of the cigarette, more sensitive in motion than breath or blood, has its waves so multitudinously inflected and reinflected, with such flights and such delays, it flows and bends upon currents of so subtle influence and impulse as to include the most active, impetuous, and lingering curls ever drawn by the finest Oriental hand--and that is not a Hindu hand, nor any hand of Aryan race. The Japanese has captured the curve of the section of a sea-wave--its flow, relaxation, and fall; but this is a single movement, whereas the line of cigarette-smoke in a still room fluctuates in twenty delicate directions. No, it is impossible to accept the saying that the poor spiral or scroll of a human design is anything but a participation in the innumerable curves and curls of nature.

Now the plaid is not only "cut off" from natural sources, as Ruskin says of Oriental design--the plaid is not only cut off from nature, and cut off from nature by the yard, for it is to be measured off in inorganic quantity; but it is even a kind of intentional contradiction of all natural or vital forms. And it is equally defiant of vital tone and of vital colour. Everywhere in nature tone is gradual, and between the fainting of a tone and the failing of a curve there is a charming analogy. But the tartan insists that its tone shall be invariable, and sharply defined by contrasts of dark and light. As to colour, it has colours, not colour.

But that plaid should now go so far afield as to decorate the noble garment of the Indies is ill news. True, Ruskin saw nothing but cruelty and corruption in Indian life or art; but let us hear an Indian maxim in regard to those who, in cruel places, are ready sufferers: "There," says the ***Mahabharata***, "where women are treated with respect, the very gods are said to be filled with joy. Women deserve to be honoured. Serve ye them. Bend your will before them. By honouring women ye are sure to attain to the fruition of all things." And the rash teachers of our youth would have persuaded us that this generous lesson was first learnt in Teutonic forests!

Nothing but extreme lowliness can well reply, or would probably be suffered to reply, to this Hindu profession of reverence. Accordingly the woman so honoured makes an offering of cakes and oil to the souls of her mother-in-law, grandmother-in-law, and great-grandmother-in-law, in gratitude for their giving her a good husband. And to go back for a moment to Ruskin's contrast of the two races, it was assuredly under the stress of some too rash reasoning that he judged the lovely art of the East as a ministrant to superstition, cruelty, and pleasure, whether wrought upon the temple, the sword, or the girdle. The innocent art of innocent Hindu women for centuries decked their most modest heads, their dedicated and sequestered beauty, their child-loving breasts, and consecrated chambers.

TWO BURDENS

One is on the breast and clings there with arms, and one on the back and clings with thongs. The burden of the back bows the body, turns the face from the sky, narrows the lungs and flattens the foot; takes away the flight and the dance from the gait of man, and ties him towards the earth--not only in the way of nature, by means of his arched feet, but by a heavy lien upon his shoulders and his brows. It is the fardel that

makes this vital figure to be subject visibly, and at several points, to
that law of gravitation which, in a state of liberty, it uses to
withstand, to countervail, to leap from, to walk with, making the
universal tether elastic. Bend in two this supple spine that can lift
itself, like a snake erect, with something better than mere balance--with
life and the active will; bend the back, and at once gravitation takes
hold of the loins and grasps the knees, and pulls upon the shoulders, and
the neck feels the weight of an abject head.

Wherever women are told off to hard open-air labour, we shall find among
them a lower class of their own kind--poorer where all are poor, and
straining at their task where all are labouring--who walk the dust with
burdens on their backs. Loads of field-labour are these, or of the
labour in a fishing-port, and large in proportion to their weight; too
large to be bound close and carried on the head, too wide to be borne on
the shoulder, too unwieldy for the clasp of arms. Among American
Indians, we are told, the women carry the tent so, and the gear of a
demenagement, and the warrior himself, upon his goods, not seldom. In
the agriculture of the European Continent the women carry the large loads
thus, the refuse is laid upon them, and all that is bound up for burning;
they are the gleaners, not of wheat but of tares. Or they carry fodder
for the imprisoned cattle, disappearing as they walk, bowed, quenched,
hooded, and hidden with hay.

Women who bear this load do not prosper. They have a downward look,
albeit not as conspirators; and in them the earth carries a burden like
their own, or but little more buoyant. Stones off the face of the stony
fields, huge sheaves of stalks and husks after granaries are filled, fuel
and forage--bent from the stature of women, those who bear those bundles
go near the earth that gave them, and breathe her dust.

In Austria, where women carry the hod and climb the ladder; in the
Rhineland, where a cart goes along the valley roads drawn by a woman

harnessed with a cow--even here I think the hardship hardly so great as where the burden is laid upon the bent back of her whose arms are too small or too weak to grasp it; for after long use in such carrying, the figure is no longer fit for habitual erection. And the use is established with those women who are so loaded. It is not that all the labouring women of such a village or such a sea-port are burdened in their turn with the burden of the back; it is rather that a class is formed, a class of the burdened and the bent; and to that class belong all ages; child-bearing women are in that sisterhood. No stronger women can be seen than the upright women of Boulogne; to whom then, but the bent, are due the many cripples, the many dwarfs, the ill-boned stragglers of that vigorous population, the many children growing awry, the many old people shuffling towards misshapen graves?

There is manifestly another burden, familiar and accustomed to the figure of woman. This does not bend her back, nor withdraw her eyes from the distance, nor rank her with the haggard waste of fields. It is borne in front, and she breasts the world with it; shoulder-high, and it is her ballast. So loaded she stands like the Dresden Raphael, and there is no bearer of sword and buckler more erect.

It is, by the way, a curious sign of indignity of race--or, if not indignity, provincialism--in the more extremely Oriental people, that a Japanese woman carries her child on her back and not upon her arm. It is a charming infant, and the mother looks no more than a gentle child; with the little creature bound to her back she carries a soft lantern in a mild blue night. She is not of a classic race, and she shuffles on her subordinate way, an irresponsible creature, who must not proffer opinions except by way of quotation, and is scarcely of the inches that measure the landscape or of the aspect that fronts the sky.

But whence is this now prevalent desire to slip the nobler and bear the ignobler burden? It is not long since an American woman wrote a book,

Women and Economics, urging equal labour upon women, by the analogy of animals that know no distinction between a strong sex and a weak, nor between a free sex and one confined to the pen, or the lair, or the cover, by the care of little ones. The reply seems too obvious that the children of men are more helpless, and are helpless for a longer time, even in proportion to their longer life, than the off-spring of other living creatures. The children of men have to be carried. This author complains that women are economically dependent upon men; and she finds that the world has "misty ideas upon the subject." If those misty ideas are to the effect that a woman who keeps house for the service of herself, her husband, and the other inmates, gives her work in return for maintenance, and is not a dependent but a colleague, I must wish that ideas "mistily" held were often so just, and ideas vaguely believed were often so well founded. Those who charge the husband with "employing" his wife choose to neglect the fact that she is mistress and hostess, as well as "servant" or "housekeeper," ministering to herself and to the guests in whose company she has pleasure, and to whose respect she has a right. Our economic author proceeds: "We are the only animal species in which the sex relation is also an economic factor. . . We have not been accustomed to face this fact beyond our loose generalization that it was 'natural,' and that other animals did so too." Has anyone really been so rash as to aver "that other animals did so too"? The obvious truth is that other animals do otherwise, but that, whatever they do, they make no rule or example for man. Again: "Whatever the economic value of the domestic industry of women is, they do not get it. The women who do the most work get the least money." And yet but now they were charged with "getting it" too dependently, or rather, with having it "got" for them by man! Is this writer indeed misled by that mere word "money," which she here lets slip?

"He nearly persuades me to go on all fours," sighs Voltaire rising--rising erect reluctantly, one may almost say--from the reading of Rousseau.

THE UNREADY

It is rashly said that the senses of children are quick. They are, on the contrary, unwieldy in turning, unready in reporting, until advancing age teaches them agility. This is not lack of sensitiveness, but mere length of process. For instance, a child nearly newly born is cruelly startled by a sudden crash in the room--a child who has never learnt to fear, and is merely overcome by the shock of sound; nevertheless, that shock of sound does not reach the conscious hearing or the nerves but after some moments, nor before some moments more is the sense of the shock expressed. The sound travels to the remoteness and seclusion of the child's consciousness, as the roar of a gun travels to listeners half a mile away.

So it is, too, with pain, which has learnt to be so instant and eager with us of later age that no point of time is lost in its touches--direct as the unintercepted message of great and candid eyes, unhampered by trivialities; even so immediate is the communication of pain. But you could count five between the prick of a surgeon's instrument upon a baby's arm and the little whimper that answers it. The child is then too young, also, to refer the feeling of pain to the arm that suffers it. Even when pain has groped its way to his mind it hardly seems to bring local tidings thither. The baby does not turn his eyes in any degree towards his arm or towards the side that is so vexed with vaccination. He looks in any other direction at haphazard, and cries at random.

See, too, how slowly the unpractised apprehension of an older child trudges after the nimbleness of a conjurer. It is the greatest failure to take these little **gobe-mouches** to a good conjurer. His successes leave them cold, for they had not yet understood what it was the good man meant to surprise them withal. The amateur it is who really astonishes them. They cannot come up even with your amateur beginner, performing at close quarters; whereas the master of his craft on a platform runs quite away at the outset from the lagging senses of his honest audience.

You may rob a child of his dearest plate at table, almost from under his ingenuous eyes, send him off in chase of it, and have it in its place and off again ten times before the little breathless boy has begun to perceive in what direction his sweets have been snatched.

Teachers of young children should therefore teach themselves a habit of awaiting, should surround themselves with pauses of patience. The simple little processes of logic that arrange the grammar of a common sentence are too quick for these young blunderers, who cannot use two pronouns but they must confuse them. I never found that a young child--one of something under nine years--was able to say, "I send them my love" at the first attempt. It will be "I send me my love," "I send them their love," "They send me my love"; not, of course, through any confusion of understanding, but because of the tardy setting of words in order with the thoughts. The child visibly grapples with the difficulty, and is beaten.

It is no doubt this unreadiness that causes little children to like twice-told tales and foregone conclusions in their games. They are not eager, for a year or two yet to come, for surprises. If you hide and they cannot see you hiding, their joy in finding you is comparatively small; but let them know perfectly well what cupboard you are in, and they will find you with shouts of discovery. The better the hiding-place is understood between you the more lively the drama. They make a convention of art for their play. The younger the children the more dramatic; and when the house is filled with outcries of laughter from the breathless breast of a child, it is that he is pretending to be surprised at finding his mother where he bade her pretend to hide. This is the comedy that never tires. Let the elder who cannot understand its charm beware how he tries to put a more intelligible form of delight in the place of it; for, if not, he will find that children also have a manner of substitution, and that they will put half-hearted laughter in the place of their natural impetuous clamours. It is certain that very young children like to play upon their own imaginations, and enjoy their own short game.

There is something so purely childlike in the delays of a child that any exercise asking for the swift apprehension of later life, for the flashes of understanding and action, from the mind and members of childhood, is no pleasure to see. The piano, for instance, as experts understand it, and even as the moderately-trained may play it, claims all the immediate action, the instantaneousness, most unnatural to childhood. There may possibly be feats of skill to which young children could be trained without this specific violence directed upon the thing characteristic of their age--their unreadiness--but virtuosity at the piano cannot be one of them. It is no delight, indeed, to see the shyness of children, or anything that is theirs, conquered and beaten; but their poor little slowness is so distinctively their own, and must needs be physiologically so proper to their years, so much a natural condition of the age of their brain, that of all childishnesses it is the one that the world should have the patience to attend upon, the humanity to foster, and the intelligence to understand.

It is true that the movements of young children are quick, but a very little attention would prove how many apparent disconnexions there are between the lively motion and the first impulse; it is not the brain that is quick. If, on a voyage in space, electricity takes thus much time, and light thus much, and sound thus much, there is one little jogging traveller that would arrive after the others had forgotten their journey, and this is the perception of a child. Surely our own memories might serve to remind us how in our childhood we inevitably missed the principal point in any procession or pageant intended by our elders to furnish us with a historical remembrance for the future. It was not our mere vagueness of understanding, it was the unwieldiness of our senses, of our reply to the suddenness of the grown up. We lived through the important moments of the passing of an Emperor at a different rate from theirs; we stared long in the wake of his Majesty, and of anything else of interest; every flash of movement, that got telegraphic answers from our parents' eyes, left us stragglers. We fell out of all ranks. Among the sights proposed for our instruction, that which befitted us best was an eclipse of the moon, done at leisure. In good time we found the moon in the sky, in good time the eclipse set in and made reasonable progress; we kept up with everything.

It is too often required of children that they should adjust themselves to the world, practised and alert. But it would be more to the purpose that the world should adjust itself to children in all its dealings with them. Those who run and keep together have to run at the pace of the tardiest. But we are apt to command instant obedience, stripped of the little pauses that a child, while very young, cannot act without. It is not a child of ten or twelve that needs them so; it is the young creature who has but lately ceased to be a baby, slow to be startled.

We have but to consider all that it implies of the loitering of senses and of an unprepared consciousness--this capacity for receiving a great shock from a noise and this perception of the shock after two or three appreciable moments--if we would know anything of the moments of a baby

Even as we must learn that our time, when it is long, is too long for children, so must we learn that our time, when it is short, is too short for them. When it is exceedingly short they cannot, without an unnatural effort, have any perception of it. When children do not see the jokes of the elderly, and disappoint expectation in other ways, only less intimate, the reason is almost always there. The child cannot turn in mid-career; he goes fast, but the impetus took place moments ago.

THE CHILD OF TUMULT

A poppy bud, packed into tight bundles by so hard and resolute a hand that the petals of the flower never afterwards lose the creases, is a type of the child. Nothing but the unfolding, which is as yet in the non-existing future, can explain the manner of the close folding of character. In both flower and child it looks much as though the process had been the reverse of what it was--as though a finished and open thing had been folded up into the bud--so plainly and certainly is the future implied, and the intention of compressing and folding-close made manifest.

With the other incidents of childish character, the crowd of impulses called "naughtiness" is perfectly perceptible--it would seem heartless to say how soon. The naughty child (who is often an angel of tenderness and charm, affectionate beyond the capacity of his fellows, and a very ascetic of penitence when the time comes) opens early his brief campaigns and raises the standard of revolt as soon as he is capable of the desperate joys of disobedience.

But even the naughty child is an individual, and must not be treated in the mass. He is numerous indeed, but not general, and to describe him you must take the unit, with all his incidents and his organic qualities as they are. Take then, for instance, one naughty child in the reality of his life. He is but six years old, slender and masculine, and not wronged by long hair, curls, or effeminate dress. His face is delicate and too often haggard with tears of penitence that Justice herself would be glad to spare him. Some beauty he has, and his mouth especially is so lovely as to seem not only angelic but itself an angel. He has absolutely no self-control and his passions find him without defence. They come upon him in the midst of his usual brilliant gaiety and cut short the frolic comedy of his fine spirits.

Then for a wild hour he is the enemy of the laws. If you imprison him, you may hear his resounding voice as he takes a running kick at the door, shouting his justification in unconquerable rage. "I'm good now!" is made as emphatic as a shot by the blow of his heel upon the panel. But if the moment of forgiveness is deferred, in the hope of a more promising repentance, it is only too likely that he will betake himself to a hostile silence and use all the revenge yet known to his imagination. "Darling mother, open the door!" cries his touching voice at last; but if the answer should be "I must leave you for a short time, for punishment," the storm suddenly thunders again. "There (crash!) I have broken a plate, and I'm glad it is broken into such little pieces that you can't mend it. I'm going to break the 'lectric light." When things are at this pass there is one way, and only one, to bring the child to an overwhelming change of mind; but it is a way that would be cruel, used more than twice or thrice in his whole career of tempest and defiance. This is to let him see that his mother is troubled. "Oh, don't cry! Oh, don't be sad!" he roars, unable still to deal with his own passionate anger, which is still dealing with him. With his kicks of rage he suddenly mingles a dance of apprehension lest his mother should have tears in her eyes. Even while he is still explicitly impenitent and defiant he tries to pull her round to the light that he may see her face. It is but a moment before the other passion of remorse comes to make havoc of the helpless child, and the first passion of anger is quelled outright.

Only to a trivial eye is there nothing tragic in the sight of these great passions within the small frame, the small will, and, in a word, the small nature. When a large and sombre fate befalls a little nature, and the stage is too narrow for the action of a tragedy, the disproportion has sometimes made a mute and unexpressed history of actual life or sometimes a famous book; it is the manifest core of George Eliot's story of ***Adam Bede***, where the suffering of Hetty is, as it were, the eye of the storm. All is expressive around her, but she is hardly articulate; the book is full of words--preachings, speeches, daily talk, aphorisms, but a space of silence remains about her in the midst of the story. And the disproportion of passion--the inner disproportion--is at least as tragic as that disproportion of fate and action; it is less intelligible, and leads into the intricacies of nature which are more difficult than the turn of events.

It seems, then, that this passionate play is acted within the narrow limits of a child's nature far oftener than in those of an adult and finally formed nature. And this, evidently, because there is unequal force at work within a child, unequal growth and a jostling of powers and energies that are hurrying to their development and pressing for exercise and life. It is this helpless inequality--this untimeliness--that makes the guileless comedy mingling with the tragedies of a poor child's day. He knows thus much--that life is troubled around him and that the fates are strong. He implicitly confesses "the strong hours" of antique song. This same boy--the tempestuous child of passion and revolt--went out with quiet cheerfulness for a walk lately, saying as his cap was put on, "Now, mother, you are going to have a little peace." This way of accepting his own conditions is shared by a sister, a very little older, who, being of an equal and gentle temper, indisposed to violence of every kind and tender to all without disquiet, observes the boy's brief frenzies as a citizen observes the climate. She knows the signs quite well and can at any time give the explanation of some particular outburst, but without any attempt to go in search of further or more original causes. Still less is she moved by the virtuous indignation that is the least charming of the ways of some little girls. ***Elle ne fait que constater***.

Her equanimity has never been overset by the wildest of his moments, and she has witnessed them all. It is needless to say that she is not frightened by his drama, for Nature takes care that her young creatures shall not be injured by sympathies. Nature encloses them in the innocent indifference that preserves their brains from the more harassing kinds of distress.

Even the very frenzy of rage does not long dim or depress the boy. It is his repentance that makes him pale, and Nature here has been rather forced, perhaps--with no very good result. Often must a mother wish that she might for a few years govern her child (as far as he is governable) by the lowest motives--trivial punishments and paltry rewards--rather than by any kind of appeal to his sensibilities. She would wish to keep the words "right" and "wrong" away from his childish ears, but in this she is not seconded by her lieutenants. The child himself is quite willing to close with her plans, in so far as he is able, and is reasonably interested in the results of her experiments. He wishes her attempts in his regard to have a fair chance. "Let's hope I'll be good all to-morrow," he says with the peculiar cheerfulness of his ordinary voice. "I do hope so, old man." "Then I'll get my penny. Mother, I was only naughty once yesterday; if I have only one naughtiness to-morrow, will you give me a halfpenny?" "No reward except for real goodness all day long." "All right."

It is only too probable that this system (adopted only after the failure of other ways of reform) will be greatly disapproved as one of bribery. It may, however, be curiously inquired whether all kinds of reward might not equally be burlesqued by that word, and whether any government, spiritual or civil, has ever even professed to deny rewards. Moreover, those who would not give a child a penny for being good will not hesitate to fine him a penny for being naughty, and rewards and punishments must stand or fall together. The more logical objection will be that goodness is ideally the normal condition, and that it should have, therefore, no explicit extraordinary result, whereas naughtiness, being abnormal, should have a visible and unusual sequel. To this the rewarding mother may reply that it is not reasonable to take "goodness" in a little child of strong passions as the normal condition. The natural thing for him is to give full sway to impulses that are so violent as to overbear his powers.

But, after all, the controversy returns to the point of practice. What is the thought, or threat, or promise that will stimulate the weak will of the child, in the moment of rage and anger, to make a sufficient resistance? If the will were naturally as well developed as the passions, the stand would be soon made and soon successful; but as it is there must needs be a bracing by the suggestion of joy or fear. Let, then, the stimulus be of a mild and strong kind at once, and mingled with the thought of distant pleasure. To meet the suffering of rage and frenzy by the suffering of fear is assuredly to make of the little unquiet mind a battle-place of feelings too hurtfully tragic. The penny is mild and strong at once, with its still distant but certain joys of purchase; the promise and hope break the mood of misery, and the will takes heart to resist and conquer.

It is only in the lesser naughtiness that he is master of himself. The lesser the evil fit the more deliberate. So that his mother, knowing herself to be not greatly feared, once tried to mimic the father's voice with a menacing, "What's that noise?" The child was persistently crying and roaring on an upper floor, in contumacy against his French nurse, when the baritone and threatening question was sent pealing up the stairs. The child was heard to pause and listen and then to say to his nurse, "Ce n'est pas Monsieur; c'est Madame," and then, without further loss of time, to resume the interrupted clamours.

Obviously, with a little creature of six years, there are two things mainly to be done--to keep the delicate brain from the evil of the present excitement, especially the excitement of painful feeling, and to break the habit of passion. Now that we know how certainly the special cells of the brain which are locally affected by pain and anger become hypertrophied by so much use, and all too ready for use in the future at the slightest stimulus, we can no longer slight the importance of habit. Any means, then, that can succeed in separating a little child from the habit of anger does fruitful work for him in the helpless time of his childhood. The work is not easy, but a little thought should make it easy for the elders to avoid the provocation which they--who should ward off provocations--are apt to bring about by sheer carelessness. It is only in childhood that our race knows such physical abandonment to sorrow and tears, as a child's despair; and the theatre with us must needs copy childhood if it would catch the note and action of a creature without hope.

THE CHILD OF SUBSIDING TUMULT

There is a certain year that is winged, as it were, against the flight of time; it does so move, and yet withstands time's movement. It is full of pauses that are due to the energy of change, has bounds and rebounds, and when it is most active then it is longest. It is not long with languor. It has room for remoteness, and leisure for oblivion. It takes great excursions against time, and travels so as to enlarge its hours. This certain year is any one of the early years of fully conscious life, and therefore it is of all the dates. The child of Tumult has been living amply and changefully through such a year--his eighth. It is difficult to believe that his is a year of the self-same date as that of the adult, the men who do not breast their days.

For them is the inelastic, or but slightly elastic, movement of things. Month matched with month shows a fairly equal length. Men and women never travel far from yesterday; nor is their morrow in a distant light. There is recognition and familiarity between their seasons. But the Child of Tumult has infinite prospects in his year. Forgetfulness and surprise set his east and his west at immeasurable distance. His Lethe runs in the cheerful sun. You look on your own little adult year, and in imagination enlarge it, because you know it to be the contemporary of his. Even she who is quite old, if she have a vital fancy, may face a strange and great extent of a few years of her life still to come--his years, the years she is to live at his side.

Reason seems to be making good her rule in this little boy's life, not so much by slow degrees as by sudden and fitful accessions. His speech is yet so childish that he chooses, for a toy, with blushes of pleasure, "a little duck what can walk"; but with a beautifully clear accent he greets his mother with the colloquial question, "Well, darling, do you know the latest?" "The *what*?" "The latest: do you know the latest?" And then he tells his news, generally, it must be owned, with some reference to his own wrongs. On another occasion the unexpected little phrase was varied; the news of the war then raging distressed him; a thousand of the side he favoured had fallen. The child then came to his mother's room with the question: "Have you heard the saddest?" Moreover the "saddest" caused him several fits of perfectly silent tears, which seized him during the day, on his walks or at other moments of recollection. From such great causes arise such little things! Some of his grief was for the nation he admired, and some was for the triumph of his brother, whose sympathies were on the other side, and who perhaps did not spare his sensibilities.

The tumults of a little child's passions of anger and grief, growing fewer as he grows older, rather increase than lessen in their painfulness. There is a fuller consciousness of complete capitulation of

all the childish powers to the overwhelming compulsion of anger. This is
not temptation; the word is too weak for the assault of a child's passion
upon his will. That little will is taken captive entirely, and before
the child was seven he knew that it was so. Such a consciousness leaves
all babyhood behind and condemns the child to suffer. For a certain
passage of his life he is neither unconscious of evil, as he was, nor
strong enough to resist it, as he will be. The time of the subsiding of
the tumult is by no means the least pitiable of the phases of human life.
Happily the recovery from each trouble is ready and sure; so that the
child who had been abandoned to naughtiness with all his will in an
entire consent to the gloomy possession of his anger, and who had later
undergone a haggard repentance, has his captivity suddenly turned again,
"like rivers in the south." "Forget it," he had wept, in a kind of
extremity of remorse; "forget it, darling, and don't, don't be sad;" and
it is he, happily, who forgets. The wasted look of his pale face is
effaced by the touch of a single cheerful thought, and five short minutes
can restore the ruin, as though a broken little German town should in the
twinkling of an eye be restored as no architect could restore it--should
be made fresh, strong, and tight again, looking like a full box of toys,
as a town was wont to look in the new days of old.

When his ruthless angers are not in possession the child shows the growth
of this tardy reason that--quickened--is hereafter to do so much for his
peace and dignity, by the sweetest consideration. Denied a second
handful of strawberries, and seeing quite clearly that the denial was
enforced reluctantly, he makes haste to reply, "It doesn't matter,
darling." At any sudden noise in the house his beautiful voice, with all
its little difficulties of pronunciation, is heard with the sedulous
reassurance: "It's all right, mother, nobody hurted ourselves!" He is
not surprised so as to forget this gentle little duty, which was never
required of him, but is of his own devising.

According to the opinion of his dear and admired American friend, he says all these things, good and evil, with an English accent; and at the American play his English accent was irrepressible. "It's too comic; no, it's too comic," he called in his enjoyment; being the only perfectly fearless child in the world, he will not consent to the conventional shyness in public, whether he be the member of an audience or of a congregation, but makes himself perceptible. And even when he has a desperate thing to say, in the moment of absolute revolt--such a thing as "I *can't* like you, mother," which anon he will recant with convulsions of distress--he has to "speak the thing he will," and when he recants it is not for fear.

If such a child could be ruled (or approximately ruled, for inquisitorial government could hardly be so much as attempted) by some small means adapted to his size and to his physical aspect, it would be well for his health, but that seems at times impossible. By no effort can his elders altogether succeed in keeping tragedy out of the life that is so unready for it. Against great emotions no one can defend him by any forethought. He is their subject; and to see him thus devoted and thus wrung, thus wrecked by tempests inwardly, so that you feel grief has him actually by the heart, recalls the reluctance--the question--wherewith you perceive the interior grief of poetry or of a devout life. Cannot the Muse, cannot the Saint, you ask, live with something less than this? If this is the truer life, it seems hardly supportable. In like manner it should be possible for a child of seven to come through his childhood with griefs that should not so closely involve him, but should deal with the easier sentiments.

Despite all his simplicity, the child has (by way of inheritance, for he has never heard them) the self-excusing fictions of our race. Accused of certain acts of violence, and unable to rebut the charge with any effect, he flies to the old convention: "I didn't know what I was doing," he avers, using a great deal of gesticulation to express the temporary distraction of his mind. "Darling, after nurse slapped me as hard as she could, I didn't know what I was doing, so I suppose I pushed her with my foot." His mother knows as well as does Tolstoi that men and children know what they are doing, and are the more intently aware as the stress of feeling makes the moments more tense; and she will not admit a plea which her child might have learned from the undramatic authors he has never read.

Far from repenting of her old system of rewards, and far from taking fright at the name of a bribe, the mother of the Child of Tumult has only to wish she had at command rewards ample and varied enough to give the shock of hope and promise to the heart of the little boy, and change his passion at its height.

www.bookjungle.com *email: sales@bookjungle.com fax: 630-214-0564 mail: Book Jungle PO Box 2226 Champaign, IL 61825*

The Codes Of Hammurabi And Moses
W. W. Davies

QTY

The discovery of the Hammurabi Code is one of the greatest achievements of archaeology, and is of paramount interest, not only to the student of the Bible, but also to all those interested in ancient history...

Religion   **ISBN:** *1-59462-338-4*   Pages:132
MSRP $12.95

The Theory of Moral Sentiments
Adam Smith

QTY

This work from 1749. contains original theories of conscience amd moral judgment and it is the foundation for systemof morals.

Philosophy   **ISBN:** *1-59462-777-0*   Pages:536
MSRP $19.95

Jessica's First Prayer
Hesba Stretton

QTY

In a screened and secluded corner of one of the many railway-bridges which span the streets of London there could be seen a few years ago, from five o'clock every morning until half past eight, a tidily set-out coffee-stall, consisting of a trestle and board, upon which stood two large tin cans, with a small fire of charcoal burning under each so as to keep the coffee boiling during the early hours of the morning when the work-people were thronging into the city on their way to their daily toil...

Childrens   **ISBN:** *1-59462-373-2*   Pages:84
MSRP $9.95

My Life and Work
Henry Ford

QTY

Henry Ford revolutionized the world with his implementation of mass production for the Model T automobile. Gain valuable business insight into his life and work with his own auto-biography... "We have only started on our development of our country we have not as yet, with all our talk of wonderful progress, done more than scratch the surface. The progress has been wonderful enough but..."

Biographies/   **ISBN:** *1-59462-198-5*   Pages:300
MSRP $21.95

www.bookjungle.com email: sales@bookjungle.com fax: 630-214-0564 mail: Book Jungle PO Box 2226 Champaign, IL 61825

The Art of Cross-Examination
Francis Wellman

QTY

I presume it is the experience of every author, after his first book is published upon an important subject, to be almost overwhelmed with a wealth of ideas and illustrations which could readily have been included in his book, and which to his own mind, at least, seem to make a second edition inevitable. Such certainly was the case with me; and when the first edition had reached its sixth impression in five months, I rejoiced to learn that it seemed to my publishers that the book had met with a sufficiently favorable reception to justify a second and considerably enlarged edition. ..

Reference   ISBN: *1-59462-647-2*   **Pages:412**
                                      MSRP $19.95

On the Duty of Civil Disobedience
Henry David Thoreau

QTY

Thoreau wrote his famous essay, On the Duty of Civil Disobedience, as a protest against an unjust but popular war and the immoral but popular institution of slave-owning. He did more than write—he declined to pay his taxes, and was hauled off to gaol in consequence. Who can say how much this refusal of his hastened the end of the war and of slavery ?

Law   ISBN: *1-59462-747-9*   **Pages:48**
                                 MSRP $7.45

Dream Psychology Psychoanalysis for Beginners
Sigmund Freud

QTY

Sigmund Freud, born Sigismund Schlomo Freud (May 6, 1856 - September 23, 1939), was a Jewish-Austrian neurologist and psychiatrist who co-founded the psychoanalytic school of psychology. Freud is best known for his theories of the unconscious mind, especially involving the mechanism of repression; his redefinition of sexual desire as mobile and directed towards a wide variety of objects; and his therapeutic techniques, especially his understanding of transference in the therapeutic relationship and the presumed value of dreams as sources of insight into unconscious desires.

Psychology   ISBN: *1-59462-905-6*   **Pages:196**
                                        MSRP $15.45

The Miracle of Right Thought
Orison Swett Marden

QTY

Believe with all of your heart that you will do what you were made to do. When the mind has once formed the habit of holding cheerful, happy, prosperous pictures, it will not be easy to form the opposite habit. It does not matter how improbable or how far away this realization may see, or how dark the prospects may be, if we visualize them as best we can, as vividly as possible, hold tenaciously to them and vigorously struggle to attain them, they will gradually become actualized, realized in the life. But a desire, a longing without endeavor, a yearning abandoned or held indifferently will vanish without realization.

Self Help   ISBN: *1-59462-644-8*   **Pages:360**
                                       MSRP $25.45

www.bookjungle.com *email: sales@bookjungle.com fax: 630-214-0564 mail: Book Jungle PO Box 2226 Champaign, IL 61825*

QTY

	Title	ISBN	Price
☐	**The Rosicrucian Cosmo-Conception Mystic Christianity** by *Max Heindel*	ISBN: *1-59462-188-8*	**$38.95**
	The Rosicrucian Cosmo-conception is not dogmatic, neither does it appeal to any other authority than the reason of the student. It is: not controversial, but is: sent forth in the, hope that it may help to clear...		*New Age/Religion Pages 646*
☐	**Abandonment To Divine Providence** by *Jean-Pierre de Caussade*	ISBN: *1-59462-228-0*	**$25.95**
	"The Rev. Jean Pierre de Caussade was one of the most remarkable spiritual writers of the Society of Jesus in France in the 18th Century. His death took place at Toulouse in 1751. His works have gone through many editions and have been republished...		*Inspirational/Religion Pages 400*
☐	**Mental Chemistry** by *Charles Haanel*	ISBN: *1-59462-192-6*	**$23.95**
	Mental Chemistry allows the change of material conditions by combining and appropriately utilizing the power of the mind. Much like applied chemistry creates something new and unique out of careful combinations of chemicals the mastery of mental chemistry...		*New Age Pages 354*
☐	**The Letters of Robert Browning and Elizabeth Barret Barrett 1845-1846 vol II** by *Robert Browning* and *Elizabeth Barrett*	ISBN: *1-59462-193-4*	**$35.95**
			Biographies Pages 596
☐	**Gleanings In Genesis (volume I)** by *Arthur W. Pink*	ISBN: *1-59462-130-6*	**$27.45**
	Appropriately has Genesis been termed "the seed plot of the Bible" for in it we have, in germ form, almost all of the great doctrines which are afterwards fully developed in the books of Scripture which follow...		*Religion/Inspirational Pages 420*
☐	**The Master Key** by *L. W. de Laurence*	ISBN: *1-59462-001-6*	**$30.95**
	In no branch of human knowledge has there been a more lively increase of the spirit of research during the past few years than in the study of Psychology, Concentration and Mental Discipline. The requests for authentic lessons in Thought Control, Mental Discipline and...		*New Age/Business Pages 422*
☐	**The Lesser Key Of Solomon Goetia** by *L. W. de Laurence*	ISBN: *1-59462-092-X*	**$9.95**
	This translation of the first book of the "Lernegton" is now for the first time made accessible to students of Talismanic Magic was done, after careful collation and edition, from numerous Ancient Manuscripts in Hebrew, Latin, and French...		*New Age/Occult Pages 92*
☐	**Rubaiyat Of Omar Khayyam** by *Edward Fitzgerald*	ISBN: *1-59462-332-5*	**$13.95**
	Edward Fitzgerald, whom the world has already learned, in spite of his own efforts to remain within the shadow of anonymity, to look upon as one of the rarest poets of the century, was born at Bredfield, in Suffolk, on the 31st of March, 1809. He was the third son of John Purcell...		*Music Pages 172*
☐	**Ancient Law** by *Henry Maine*	ISBN: *1-59462-128-4*	**$29.95**
	The chief object of the following pages is to indicate some of the earliest ideas of mankind, as they are reflected in Ancient Law, and to point out the relation of those ideas to modern thought.		*Religion/History Pages 452*
☐	**Far-Away Stories** by *William J. Locke*	ISBN: *1-59462-129-2*	**$19.45**
	"Good wine needs no bush, but a collection of mixed vintages does. And this book is just such a collection. Some of the stories I do not want to remain buried for ever in the museum files of dead magazine-numbers an author's not unpardonable vanity..."		*Fiction Pages 272*
☐	**Life of David Crockett** by *David Crockett*	ISBN: *1-59462-250-7*	**$27.45**
	"Colonel David Crockett was one of the most remarkable men of the times in which he lived. Born in humble life, but gifted with a strong will, an indomitable courage, and unremitting perseverance...		*Biographies/New Age Pages 424*
☐	**Lip-Reading** by *Edward Nitchie*	ISBN: *1-59462-206-X*	**$25.95**
	Edward B. Nitchie, founder of the New York School for the Hard of Hearing, now the Nitchie School of Lip-Reading, Inc, wrote "LIP-READING Principles and Practice". The development and perfecting of this meritorious work on lip-reading was an undertaking...		*How-to Pages 400*
☐	**A Handbook of Suggestive Therapeutics, Applied Hypnotism, Psychic Science** by *Henry Munro*	ISBN: *1-59462-214-0*	**$24.95**
			Health/New Age/Health/Self-help Pages 376
☐	**A Doll's House: and Two Other Plays** by *Henrik Ibsen*	ISBN: *1-59462-112-8*	**$19.95**
	Henrik Ibsen created this classic when in revolutionary 1848 Rome. Introducing some striking concepts in playwriting for the realist genre, this play has been studied the world over.		*Fiction/Classics/Plays 308*
☐	**The Light of Asia** by *sir Edwin Arnold*	ISBN: *1-59462-204-3*	**$13.95**
	In this poetic masterpiece, Edwin Arnold describes the life and teachings of Buddha. The man who was to become known as Buddha to the world was born as Prince Gautama of India but he rejected the worldly riches and abandoned the reigns of power when...		*Religion/History/Biographies Pages 170*
☐	**The Complete Works of Guy de Maupassant** by *Guy de Maupassant*	ISBN: *1-59462-157-8*	**$16.95**
	"For days and days, nights and nights, I had dreamed of that first kiss which was to consecrate our engagement, and I knew not on what spot I should put my lips..."		*Fiction/Classics Pages 240*
☐	**The Art of Cross-Examination** by *Francis L. Wellman*	ISBN: *1-59462-309-0*	**$26.95**
	Written by a renowned trial lawyer, Wellman imparts his experience and uses case studies to explain how to use psychology to extract desired information through questioning.		*How-to/Science/Reference Pages 408*
☐	**Answered or Unanswered?** by *Louisa Vaughan*	ISBN: *1-59462-248-5*	**$10.95**
	Miracles of Faith in China		*Religion Pages 112*
☐	**The Edinburgh Lectures on Mental Science (1909)** by *Thomas*	ISBN: *1-59462-008-3*	**$11.95**
	This book contains the substance of a course of lectures recently given by the writer in the Queen Street Hall, Edinburgh. Its purpose is to indicate the Natural Principles governing the relation between Mental Action and Material Conditions...		*New Age/Psychology Pages 148*
☐	**Ayesha** by *H. Rider Haggard*	ISBN: *1-59462-301-5*	**$24.95**
	Verily and indeed it is the unexpected that happens! Probably if there was one person upon the earth from whom the Editor of this, and of a certain previous history, did not expect to hear again...		*Classics Pages 380*
☐	**Ayala's Angel** by *Anthony Trollope*	ISBN: *1-59462-352-X*	**$29.95**
	The two girls were both pretty, but Lucy who was twenty-one who supposed to be simple and comparatively unattractive, whereas Ayala was credited, as her Bombwhat romantic name might show, with poetic charm and a taste for romance. Ayala when her father died was nineteen...		*Fiction Pages 484*
☐	**The American Commonwealth** by *James Bryce*	ISBN: *1-59462-286-8*	**$34.45**
	An interpretation of American democratic political theory. It examines political mechanics and society from the perspective of Scotsman James Bryce		*Politics Pages 572*
☐	**Stories of the Pilgrims** by *Margaret P. Pumphrey*	ISBN: *1-59462-116-0*	**$17.95**
	This book explores pilgrims religious oppression in England as well as their escape to Holland and eventual crossing to America on the Mayflower, and their early days in New England...		*History Pages 268*

www.bookjungle.com *email:* sales@bookjungle.com *fax:* 630-214-0564 *mail:* Book Jungle PO Box 2226 Champaign, IL 61825

QTY

The Fasting Cure *by Sinclair Upton* ISBN: *1-59462-222-1* **$13.95**
In the Cosmopolitan Magazine for May, 1910, and in the Contemporary Review (London) for April, 1910, I published an article dealing with my experiences in fasting. I have written a great many magazine articles, but never one which attracted so much attention... *New Age/Self Help/Health Pages 164*

Hebrew Astrology *by Sepharial* ISBN: *1-59462-308-2* **$13.45**
In these days of advanced thinking it is a matter of common observation that we have left many of the old landmarks behind and that we are now pressing forward to greater heights and to a wider horizon than that which represented the mind-content of our progenitors... *Astrology Pages 144*

Thought Vibration or The Law of Attraction in the Thought World ISBN: *1-59462-127-6* **$12.95**
by William Walker Atkinson *Psychology/Religion Pages 128*

Optimism *by Helen Keller* ISBN: *1-59462-108-X* **$15.95**
Helen Keller was blind, deaf, and mute since 19 months old, yet famously learned how to overcome these handicaps, communicate with the world, and spread her lectures promoting optimism. An inspiring read for everyone... *Biographies/Inspirational Pages 84*

Sara Crewe *by Frances Burnett* ISBN: *1-59462-360-0* **$9.45**
In the first place, Miss Minchin lived in London. Her home was a large, dull, tall one, in a large, dull square, where all the houses were alike, and all the sparrows were alike, and where all the door-knockers made the same heavy sound... *Childrens/Classic Pages 88*

The Autobiography of Benjamin Franklin *by Benjamin Franklin* ISBN: *1-59462-135-7* **$24.95**
The Autobiography of Benjamin Franklin has probably been more extensively read than any other American historical work, and no other book of its kind has had such ups and downs of fortune. Franklin lived for many years in England, where he was agent... *Biographies/History Pages 332*

Name

Email

Telephone

Address

City, State ZIP

☐ Credit Card   ☐ Check / Money Order

Credit Card Number

Expiration Date

Signature

Please Mail to: Book Jungle
PO Box 2226
Champaign, IL 61825
or Fax to: 630-214-0564

ORDERING INFORMATION
web: www.bookjungle.com
email: sales@bookjungle.com
fax: 630-214-0564
mail: Book Jungle PO Box 2226 Champaign, IL 61825
or PayPal *to* sales@bookjungle.com

Please contact us for bulk discounts

DIRECT-ORDER TERMS

**20% Discount if You Order
Two or More Books**
Free Domestic Shipping!
Accepted: Master Card, Visa,
Discover, American Express

www.ingramcontent.com/pod-product-compliance
Lightning Source LLC
Chambersburg PA
CBHW081325040426
42453CB00013B/2303